THE ICSA
COMPANY
SECRETARY'S
CHECKLISTS

THE ICSA COMPANY SECRETARY'S CHECKLISTS

Sixth edition

Douglas Armour FCIS

Director
David Venus & Company Limited

ICSA Publishing Limited

Published by
ICSA Publishing Ltd
16 Park Crescent
London W1B 1AH

© ICSA Publishing Ltd, 2009

Reprinted 2010

Typeset in 10/12pt Schneidler by
Hands Fotoset, Mapperley, Nottingham

Printed and bound in Great Britain by
WM Print, Frederick Street, Walsall, WS2 9NE

British Library Cataloguing in Publication Data

A catalogue record for this book is available from the British Library.

ISBN 978-1-86072-378-0

Contents

The author

Douglas Armour has worked as a Chartered Secretary in public practice for over 24 years. He is now a director of David Venus & Company Limited, and has been and continues to be company secretary to many private companies as well as public companies whose shares are listed or admitted to AIM or PLUS.

He heads the company's share registration business carried out under the trading name SLC Registrars, which acts as registrar to Listed, AIM and PLUS companies, as well as companies both private and public with substantial numbers of shareholders.

Over the course of the last 24 years Douglas has accumulated a wealth of practical experience and has drawn on this to include in this book those procedures that company secretaries, directors and practitioners will find most useful.

As with all legislation, the provisions of the Companies Acts and related legislation are open to interpretation and must be assessed in the context of the particular circumstances at hand, the memorandum and articles of association of the company in question, and any relevant shareholders' agreement or other pertinent ancillary agreements. While every effort has been made to ensure the accuracy of the content of this book, neither the author nor the publisher can accept responsibility for any loss arising to anyone relying on the information contained herein.

This edition was written with considerable assistance from Douglas's colleagues within David Venus & Company Ltd and with the continued patience of ICSA Publishing Ltd as yet another deadline came and went without sight of the manuscript and to whom Douglas is extremely grateful.

Preface

The sixth edition of this book represents a major updating of the content, to reflect full implementation of the Companies Act 2006 as at 1 October 2009.

Please note however that at the time of writing, not all the necessary statutory instruments associated with the final implementation had been passed into law and accordingly the reader will need to carefully check the actual orders made in respect of the topics on accounts for an oversea company and the schedule of sensitive words.

The ICSA Company Secretary's Checklists provides a handy, quick-reference guide to the more common company secretarial procedures. The book is not intended to be a legal reference book, and accordingly little explanation of the relevant legislation is made. As more detailed information will often be required, the book has been cross-referenced to the relevant legislation, *The ICSA Company Secretary's Handbook* (7th edition) and *Company Secretarial Practice: The Manual of the Institute of Chartered Secretaries and Administrators*, both of which are published by ICSA Publishing.

Each topic comprises a general commentary on the particular matter, checklist of items to be considered, procedural steps to be taken, Companies House filing requirements, as well as general notes and cross-references.

The Companies House references are to their series of guidance booklets which are available on request by post or may be downloaded from the Companies House website (www.companieshouse.gov.uk).

These checklists should not be regarded as exhaustive, to be followed in all circumstances, but serve as a guide to the reader, indicating procedures that should be considered in the context of the matter at hand.

Although, overall, the checklists have been prepared with private companies in mind, many of the procedures are equally applicable, and in some cases only applicable, to public companies.

The book will be of particular interest to:

- *Accountants/auditors*. Many private company directors will turn to their accountant for advice on company secretarial matters. This book sets out answers to the majority of procedural queries likely to be raised.
- *Solicitors/chartered secretary practices*. While most solicitors and chartered secretaries will have access to extensive libraries of legal reference books, these are often too detailed for quick reference. This book is intended to complement rather than duplicate existing reference sources.
- *Company secretaries/directors*. Company secretaries will find this book of particular use when advising their directors on particular matters, even if advice will ultimately be sought from the company's professional advisers. An understanding of the practical issues for any particular matter will facilitate proper discussion at board level, collation of relevant information, and the issuing of coherent instructions to professional advisers.

Douglas Armour
July 2009

Abbreviations

AIM	Alternative Investment Market
BNA 1985	Business Names Act 1985
CA 1985	Companies Act 1985
CA 2006/the Act	Companies Act 2006
CBNR 1981	Company and Business Names Regulations 1981
CC	Combined Code
CDDA 1986	Company Directors Disqualification Act 1986
CSP	Company Secretarial Practice, the official ICSA information service
EA 2002	Enterprise Act 2002
EEIG	European Economic Interest Group
FSA	Financial Services Authority
FSMA	2000 Financial Services and Markets Act 2000
Handbook	ICSA Company Secretary's Handbook
IA 1986	Insolvency Act 1986
ICSA/The Institute	The Institute of Chartered Secretaries and Administrators
IR 1986	Insolvency Rules 1986
LLP	Limited Liability Partnership
LR	Listing Rules
NED	Non-Executive Director
UKLA	UK Listing Authority
USR 2001	Uncertificated Securities Regulations 2001

Statute references are to the Companies Act 2006 unless otherwise stated.

Accounting reference date

All companies, whether trading or not, must prepare accounts and file a copy with the Registrar of Companies. The accounts are prepared in respect of each accounting period. Accounting periods begin at the conclusion of the previous period, or the date of incorporation, and end on the accounting reference date. Companies may choose an accounting reference date. If no alternative date is chosen the company's accounting reference date will be the last day of the month of the incorporation. s.394 s.390 s.391(4) s.392

A company may change its accounting reference date at any time provided the filing date for the current or new period has not expired. An accounting reference period may not exceed 18 months and, except in certain circumstances, a company may not extend its accounting period twice in any five-year period. s.392(3)

A company may extend its accounting period more than once in any five-year period of it changing to fall in line with the accounting reference date of a holding or subsidiary company or if the company is in administration.

Checklist

- The filing period for the current year must not have expired. s.392(4)
- The filing period for the proposed new period must not have expired. s.394(5)
- The new period must not be longer than 18 months, unless an administration order is in force. s.394(5)
- If extending the period, the company must not previously have extended its accounting year end in the previous five years, or if it has, the change must be justified. s.394(3)
- If the new year end has already passed, can accounts to that date be prepared (i.e. stocktakes, asset valuation, etc.)?
- Directors' resolution is required either at a meeting or by written resolution.
- File form AA01. s.392(1)

Procedure

- Convene a directors' meeting to authorise the change in accounting year.
- Form AA01 must be filed at Companies House.

Filing requirement

- Form AA01.

Notes

- The company's first accounting period must be longer than six months, but not longer than 18 months, starting from the date of incorporation. The first accounting period begins with the date of incorporation even if the company does not immediately commence trading. — s.391(5) s.390(2)
- The second and subsequent accounting periods may be as short as the directors wish, but may not exceed 18 months. — s.392(5)
- A company can extend its accounting year only once in any five-year period, unless the accounting period is being changed to coincide with that of its holding company or any subsidiary. The accounting period can be shortened as many times as required. — s.392(3)
- The length of any accounting period, even one that has ended, can be altered, provided that the relevant form is received by the Registrar before the end of the period in which the accounts for that the current or proposed period must be filed. The change in year-end will become effective once the Registrar of Companies has received the appropriate form. — s.392(1)
- Directors wishing to extend the accounting period must first confirm that the accounting year-end has not been extended in the previous five years.
- The date by which accounts must be submitted to the Registrar may be shortened when the accounting period is for a period of less than 12 months (see page 5).
- Normally a private company has nine months from its accounting reference date to file its accounts. For a public company the period is six months. — s.442
- Companies can make their accounts up to any date within seven days of the actual accounting reference date. This is to enable companies to undertake stocktakes outside normal business hours without needing to change their year end. — s.390(2)(b)
- Companies may apply for an extension to the filing deadline provided this is received by the Registrar prior to the filing deadline, however there need to be exceptional circumstances in order to be granted an extension. — s.442(5)

- In addition to notifying the Registrar of Companies, the directors may also consider notifying the following: bankers, auditors, accountants, HM Revenue & Customs, subsidiaries, joint venture partners, London Stock Exchange (if listed).

More information

Handbook: Chapters 10 and 14. Manual: Chapter 16.

Accounts – approval

Accounts, whether audited or not, must be prepared and approved by the board of directors and issued to the members.

ss.394, 414, 423

Although members of a public company consider and receive the accounts in general meeting and can vote on whether or not to accept them, they do not, strictly speaking, approve them. If the members reject them, the directors are not obliged to amend the accounts unless they contain a factual error. However, non-acceptance of accounts will be regarded as a vote of no confidence in the board.

s.434

Checklist

- Convene a directors' meeting for directors to approve the accounts. Ensure valid quorum present.

  s.414(1)

- The directors' report must be signed by a director or by the company secretary.

  s.419(1)
  s.433
  ss.420, 422

- Quoted companies must prepare a directors' remuneration report which must be signed by a director or the company secretary (see page 72).

  s.433

- The balance sheet must be signed by at least one director; the name(s) of the signing director(s) must be shown together with the date of approval.

  s.414(2)
  s.433

- If audited, the audit report must be signed by the auditors and the date of approval shown. If the auditors are a firm the audit report must be signed by the senior statutory auditor who must sign in their own name on behalf of the firm and their name must be shown. The name of the senior statutory auditor may be omitted if there are concerns over safety.

  ss.503–505
  s.506

- Full accounts must be issued to all members entitled to receive notice of and vote at general meetings. In the case of a private company it must send out its accounts to members before the end of the period allowed for filing the accounts (usually nine months (see page 5). In the case of a public company the accounts must be sent out at least 21 days before the date of the meeting to receive them.

  s.423
  s.424

- Full or abbreviated accounts must be filed at Companies House by the due date, see page 1.

  ss.441, 442

Procedure

- Convene a directors' meeting to consider the accounts and to convene a general meeting. Ensure valid quorum present.
- Final draft of the accounts to be approved by the directors.
- The directors' report and the balance sheet must be signed. The directors' report can be signed by the company secretary or a director; however, the balance sheet *must* be signed by at least one director. The published accounts must include the names of the director and/or company secretary who have signed the balance sheet and directors' report.
- A quoted company must prepare a directors' remuneration report, which must be signed by a director or the company secretary.
- The same director can sign the directors' report, directors' remuneration report (if any) and the balance sheet.
- If the accounts are audited, signed copies must be returned to the auditors so that the audit report can be signed.
- One signed copy of the accounts must be filed with the Registrar of Companies within the appropriate period (see below).
- Copies of the accounts must be sent to the shareholders and a general meeting of the shareholders convened, for the shareholders to consider the accounts, within nine months of the year-end for a private company and six months for a public company. Private companies are exempted from the obligation to convene a shareholders' meeting unless required to do so by their articles of association (see page 32).   s.442
- Companies, if authorised to do so by their shareholders, may issue summary financial statements to the shareholders, provided that the full accounts are made available on request.   s.426
- Certain companies may file abbreviated accounts with the Registrar of Companies (see pages 14 and 18).   s.441
- Full accounts will be required for issue to the shareholders and to HM Revenue & Customs.
- Additional copies will normally be sent to the company's bankers.
- The usual period for delivery of accounts to the Registrar is nine months from the end of the accounting period for a private company, and six months for a public company. However, if the accounts are the first accounts and are for a period of more than 12 months, the accounts must be submitted no later than nine months (six months for a public company) from the first anniversary of incorporation, or three months from the end of the period, whichever expires later.   s.442   s.442(3)
- Where the accounting period has been shortened, the period for   s.442(4)

delivery of the accounts is nine months for private companies and six months for public companies from the end of the period, or three months from the date of notice, whichever expires later.

■ The Registrar of Companies imposes penalties for late sub-   s.453
mission of accounts. When setting the accounting reference date, care must be taken to ensure that the accounts can be prepared in time to submit them to the Registrar of Companies (see page 1).

Filing requirement

■ Full or abbreviated copy of the accounts within 21 months of the start of the accounting period for a private company (usually nine months after year end) and within 18 months of the start of the accounting period for a public company (usually six months after the year end).

Notes

■ Accounts must have original signatures on the directors' report, directors' remuneration report, audit report, if audited, and balance sheet.
■ The name of the person signing must be shown.
■ The company registration number must be shown on the first page.
■ As the Registrar will unbind and discard any folder, an unbound copy of the accounts should be filed.
■ The accounts must be legible and be capable of being digitally scanned. Accordingly, it is best to file typed accounts printed on plain paper. Accounts printed on coloured or glossy paper or with graphics may be rejected as illegible.
■ As the accounts are not subject to shareholder approval it is not necessary to wait until after the general meeting at which the accounts are received by shareholders before filing a copy of the accounts with the Registrar of Companies.
■ The period allowed for filing the accounts was shortened by the CA 2006 and the old, longer, filing period applies to accounting periods beginning on or before 5 April 2008.

More information

Handbook: Chapter 9. Manual: Chapters 14 and 16.

Accounts – directors' remuneration report

Directors of listed companies are required to include in the annual report and accounts a remuneration report. The report must also comply with the Listing Rules and the Combined Code, or where the provisions of the Combined Code are not complied with, a statement of those provisions not complied with and the explanation for such departure must be included.

s.420

CC section 1

Checklist

- Report must be approved by the directors and signed by a director or the company secretary.
- Report should contain details for all person who were directors at any time during the financial year being reported on.
- Report must comply with schedule A of the Combined Code (see below).

s.422

para.6 Sch.8, SI2008/410

CC B1.1

Committee

- Has the board complied with the Combined Code provisions in all respects, or explained any provisions not complied with?
- Does the report explain the company's approach to the combined code?
- Does the remuneration committee comprise only independent non-executive directors?
- If there is a report of the remuneration committee, does it identify the members of the committee, the number of committee meetings and number of meetings attended by each member?

para.2 Sch.8, SI 2008/410

CC A1.2

Policy statement

- Is there a statement that the remuneration committee has given due consideration to the combined code in forming the company's remuneration policy?
- Is there a statement of the directors' policy on board remuneration for the following and subsequent years?

LR 12.43A para.3(1) Sch.8, SI 2008/410

- Does the statement provide the necessary details of performance criteria for directors' share options or incentive schemes? para.3(2) Sch.8, SI 2008/410
- Where options or LTIPS are granted in a large block, has the policy been explained? CC A.5
- Have any changes in the policy from the previous year been listed and explained? para.3(2)(e) Sch.8, SI 2008/410
- Is the policy on allowing directors to take up external appointments and retain any payment explained and are the payments disclosed? LR 12.43A(c) (viii); CC B1.4
- Is the policy on the length of directors' contracts, notice periods and termination payments explained? para.3(4)6 Sch.8, SI 2008/410
- Does the report justify the inclusion of non-salary remuneration in pension earnings? LR 12.43A(c)(v)
- Does the report highlight any company specific factors in respect of total remuneration, relative levels of basic and performance-related salary and the main para.meters of any bonus scheme, including any upper cap? para.3 Sch.8, SI 2008/410 CC Sch.A
- Does the report contain a performance graph showing the total shareholder return on the company's shares during the previous five years, together with a total shareholder return on an identified peer group index? para.5 Sch.8, SI 2008/410
- For each person who served as a director at any time during the financial year, details of their service contract or contract for services including the date of the contract, unexpired term, notice period, provisions for compensation on early termination and any other details required to enable members to estimate the liability of the company in the event of early termination. para.6 Sch.8, SI 2008/410 para.7 Sch.8, SI 2008/410

Directors' remuneration

- Have the remuneration disclosure details been audited and does the audit report cover compliance with the specified disclosures? s.497 s.11(2) and (3)
- Are the following details disclosed for each person who served as a director at any time during the financial year:basic salary and fees; SI 2008/410 LR12.43A(c)(ii)
  - □ bonus payments;
  - □ expenses chargeable to UK taxation, and paid in respect of qualifying services;
  - □ compensation for loss of office, breach of contract or other termination payment;
  - □ value of benefits in kind not disclosed elsewhere;
  - □ aggregate remuneration for the previous year;
  - □ Any non-cash remuneration?
- Does the report give reasons for choosing that particular index?

Options

- Have the share option disclosure details been audited, and does the audit report cover compliance with the specified disclosures?
- Details of any options and SAYE held, showing market price at year end and exercise date covering:
  - □ number of options held at beginning of year or date of appointment;
  - □ number of options held at year end or cessation of appointment;
  - □ number of options granted, exercised or lapsed during year;
  - □ for each unexercised option held details of the exercise price, exercise period, expiry date grant price and amount paid for the award (if anything);
  - □ details of any changes to the terms and conditions of the options;
  - □ a summary of any performance criteria and any variation in the performance criteria;
  - □ market price of any options exercised (on exercise date);
  - □ market value at end of year for all unexercised options and price range during the year.
- If disclosure would result in a report of excessive length, various elements may be aggregated in accordance with para.10 Sch.8, SI 2008/410.

para.9 Sch.8, SI 2008/410

s.497 s.11(2) and (3) SI 2008/410 LR 12.43A(c)(iii)

para.11 Sch.8, SI 2008/410

LTIPs

- Have the LTIP disclosure details been audited, and does the audit report cover compliance with the specified disclosures?
- Are the details provided in a tabular format by showing for each directors and each LTIP interests at beginning and end of the year and any awards or grants made including details of any performance criteria and the period during which the criteria must be met?
- In respect of any awards vesting during the year, details of the shares, cash or other benefit received, dates of the award, monetary value at time of award and vesting, market value of any shares received at date of award and vesting and applicable performance criteria.
- Details of any LTIP applicable to only one director.

s.497 s.11(2) and (3) SI 2008/410

Retirement benefits

- Does the report contain details (by director) of the following for defined benefit schemes:
  - □ changes in accrued benefit during the year;
  - □ amount of accrued benefit at the end of the year;

para.13 Sch.8, SI 2008/410

- ☐ transfer value of the accrued benefit at the beginning and end of the year;
- ☐ the increase or decrease in transfer value after deducting contributions made during the year;
- ☐ for any money purchase scheme, the details of any contributions paid in respect of the financial year and any other financial year;
- ☐ details of any retirement benefit paid or receivable by a director of former director in excess of the benefits to which they were entitled at the date the benefits first became payable or, if later, 31 March 1997.

para.14 Sch.8, SI 2008/410

Compensation payments

para.15 Sch.8, SI 2008/410

- Details of any significant award made to any former director including any compensation in respect of loss of office and pensions not disclosed elsewhere.

Third party payments

para.16 Sch.8, SI 2008/410

- Details of any amounts paid, whether in cash or otherwise to a third party for making available the services of any person as a director or while that person is a director of the company or any subsidiaries or other undertakings at the request of the company or in connection with the management of the affairs of the company or other undertaking.

Procedure

- The contents of the remuneration report must be approved by the board at a board meeting.

s.422

- A resolution to approve the remuneration report must be put to shareholders at the same meeting at which the accounts are received by members.

s.439

Filing requirement

- To be included in the annual report and accounts filed with the Registrar of Companies.

Notes

- In addition to the Companies Act, Listing Rules and Combined Code various shareholder representative bodies have issued their own guidance on the content of the remuneration report.

More information

📖 Handbook: Chapter 10. 📓 Manual: Chapter 16.

Accounts – exemption from audit

Certain private companies and dormant public companies qualify for exemption from audit if they satisfy certain criteria. These companies do not need to apply for the exemption; they are automatically exempt if they qualify.

ss.477, 480, 482

Shareholders holding between them at least 10 per cent of the company's issued share capital, or 10 per cent of the members, in the case of a company without share capital, may give notice to the company requiring that the accounts be audited, provided that the notice is given no later than one month prior to the end of the financial year.

s.476

Checklist

■ Total exemption is available to companies that:
  □ qualify as a small company in relation to that year (see page 18);
  □ whose turnover does not exceed £6.5 million in that year; and
  □ whose balance sheet total for that year does not exceed £3.26 million.

s.477

■ A company is not entitled to exemption from audit if at any time during the financial year:
  □ it was a public company, unless it was dormant; or
  □ it was a banking or insurance company, e-money issuer, a MiFID investment firm, a UCITS management company or carries on insurance market activities; or
  □ it was a special register body or an employers association as defined in the Trade Union and Labour Relations (Consolidation) Act 1992 or the Industrial Relations (Northern Ireland) Order 1992

s.478

■ A company that is a parent or subsidiary undertaking at any time during the financial year is not entitled to exemption from audit unless:
  □ the group qualifies as small (see page 18) and was not at any time during that year an ineligible group, see below;

s.479

- □ turnover of the whole group does not exceed £6.5million net or £7.8 million gross; and
- □ the group's continued balance sheet total does not exceed £3.26 million net or £3.9 million gross.
- ■ A company that is a dormant subsidiary throughout the period is not excluded from qualifying as small under   s.479(2) s.479(3)
- ■ A group is ineligible if any member of the group is: s.384
  - □ a public company;
  - □ a corporate body whose shares are admitted to trading on a regulated market in an EEA State;
  - □ a person authorised under FSMA 2000 to carry on a regulated activity;
  - □ a small company that is an authorised insurance company, banking company, e-money issuer, MiFID investment firm or a UCITS management company; or
  - □ a person who carries on insurance market activity.

Procedure

- ■ There is no procedure: exemption is automatic if the criteria are met.

Filing requirement

- ■ Copy of the abbreviated accounts within the appropriate time-scale, usually six months for a public company or nine months for a private company (see page 5).   s.442
- ■ Copies of the full statutory accounts are still required to be circulated to members within the appropriate timescale: six months for a public company and nine months for a private company.   s.423

Notes

- ■ A company that qualifies for exemption from audit is also exempt from the obligation to appoint auditors.   ss.475, 485

More information

⬜Handbook: Chapter 10. 📘 Manual: Chapter 15.

Accounts – late filing penalties

If accounts, whether audited or dormant, are received by the Registrar of Companies after the due date for filing has passed, the company will be fined according to a sliding scale. *s.453*

It should be noted that the onus is on directors to *deliver* accounts to the Registrar of Companies within the specified time. It is not sufficient to show that they were *posted* within the specified time. Late filing penalties do not apply to annual returns. *s.441(1)*

The scale of penalties is as follows:

	Private companies	Public companies
Up to 1 month late	£150	£750
Up to 3 months late	£375	£1,500
Up to 6 months late	£750	£3,000
More than 6 months late	£1,500	£7,500

Notes

- The penalties are imposed on the company, not the directors, and are a civil matter. However, under certain circumstances the directors may also be prosecuted for failure to submit accounts on time. This is a criminal offence, and on conviction a maximum fine of £2,000 may be imposed by the court for each separate offence. *s.453* *s.451* *s.451(4)*
- Unlimited companies do not need to file copies of their accounts with the Registrar of Companies. *s.448*

More information

Handbook: Chapter 10. Manual: Chapter 16.
Companies House: Guidance booklet GBA5.

Accounts – medium-sized companies

Companies qualifying as medium-sized may file abbreviated accounts with the Registrar of Companies. ss.441(1), 445

Checklist

- In order to qualify or to be treated as qualifying as a medium-sized company in respect of any particular financial year, the company must be or have been medium-sized during one or more of the following periods:
  - if it qualifies in its first financial year; or s.465(1)
  - if it qualifies in that year and in the year before; or s.465(2)(a)
  - if it qualifies in that year and the company qualified in the year before; or s.465(2)(b)
  - if the company qualified in the preceding year and the company qualified as medium-sized in respect of that year. s.465(2)(c)
- A medium-sized company is one that meets at least two of the following requirements: s.465(3)
  - turnover not exceeding £25.9 million;
  - balance sheet total not exceeding £12.9 million;
  - average number of employees not exceeding 250.
- A company does not qualify if at any time during the financial year it was: s.467(1)
  - a public company; or
  - authorised under Part 4 FSMA 2000 to carry on a regulated activity or carries on insurance market activities; or
  - a member of an ineligible group.
- A group is ineligible if any of its members is:
  - a public company; s.467(2)
  - a corporate body whose shares are admitted to trading on a regulated market in an EEA State;
  - a person (other than a small company) authorised under FSMA 2000 to carry on a regulated activity;
  - a small company that is an authorised insurance company, banking company, e-money issuer, MiFID investment firm or a UCITS management company; or
  - a person who carries on insurance market activity.

Procedure

- The information required for abbreviated accounts of a medium-sized company is:
  - □ full balance sheet;   s.445(1)
  - □ abbreviated profit and loss account;   s.445(3)(a)
  - □ special auditors' report unless exempt from audit;   ss.449(2), (5)
  - □ directors' report;   s.445(1)
  - □ full notes.
- Additionally there must be the following notes to the accounts:
  - □ A statement above the director's signature on the Balance   s.450(3)
    Sheet that the directors' accounts have relied on the
    exemptions for individual accounts on the grounds that the
    company is entitled to benefit from those exemptions as a
    medium-sized company.

Filing requirement

- Copy of the abbreviated accounts within the appropriate time-   s.442
  scale, usually six months for a public company or nine months
  for a private company (see page 5).

Notes

- With the exception of the profit and loss account, abbreviated
  medium-sized accounts are the same as full accounts, and so
  there is little practical benefit from utilising the exemption.
- Copies of the full statutory accounts are still required to be circu-   s.423
  lated to members within the appropriate timescale: six months
  for a public company and nine months for a private company.

More information

Handbook: Chapter 10. Manual: Chapter 16.
Companies House: Guidance booklet GBA3.

Accounts – oversea companies

Branches of an oversea company whose governing law requires the publication of audited accounts must deliver a copy of those accounts to the Registrar of Companies within three months of their publication, together with a certified translation if the original is not in English. This applies to all companies incorporated within the European Economic Area.

s.699AA,
Sch.21D 2(2)

Sch.21D 2(4)

Sch.21D 2(3)

Oversea companies cannot file abbreviated accounts unless their governing legislation permits the filing of modified accounts, in which case those accounts shall be filed.

ss.699AA,
699B, 700

All oversea companies with a place of business, and any overseas companies with a branch, whose governing legislation does not require publication of audited accounts must prepare and file accounts drawn up in accordance with s.700.

Sch.21D 7

Checklist

s.699A companies

- Is the company registered as a branch?
- Does the legislation in its country of incorporation require the publication of audited accounts?

s.700 accounts

- Prepare audited accounts in accordance s.700.
- Accounts must be for the whole company, not just the place of business or branch.

Filing requirement

- Copy of accounts under s.690A within three months of publication together with certified translation if required; or
- copy of accounts under s.700 within 13 months of year end. These need not include directors' or auditors' reports, information relating to turnover, UK taxation, subsidiaries, directors' emoluments and loans to directors.
- Filing fee £15.

Sch.21D
ss 2(2), 2(4)
s.702

SI 1990/440

Notes

- Different rules (not dealt with here) apply to oversea credit or financial institutions.
- The exemptions available to small and medium-sized companies and dormant companies are not available to oversea companies.
- Although oversea companies which are required to prepare accounts in accordance with s.700 are subject to the same rules regarding accounting reference dates (see page 1) as non-oversea companies they may extend their year ends as many times as they wish.

More information

Handbook: Chapter 21. Manual: Chapter 16.
Companies House: GBO1.

Accounts – small-sized companies

Companies qualifying as small-sized may file abbreviated accounts with the Registrar of Companies.

ss.441(1)
444, 444A

Checklist

- In order to qualify or to be treated as qualifying as a small-sized company in respect of any particular financial year, the company must be or must have been small-sized during one or more of the following periods:
  - ☐ if it qualifies in its first financial year; or
  - ☐ if it qualifies in that year and in the year before; or
  - ☐ if it qualifies in that year and the company qualified in the year before; or
  - ☐ if the qualifying conditions were met in the preceding year and the company qualified as small-sized in respect of that year.

  s.382(1)
  s.382(2)(a)
  s.382(2)(b)

  s.382(2)(c)

  s.382(3)

- A small-sized company is one that meets at least two of the following requirements:
  - ☐ turnover not exceeding £6.5 million;
  - ☐ balance sheet total not exceeding £3.26 million;
  - ☐ average number of employees not exceeding 50.

  s.384(1)

- A company does not qualify if at any time during the financial year it was:
  - ☐ a public company; or
  - ☐ an authorised insurance company, banking company, e-money issuer, MiFID investment firm or a UCITS management company; or
  - ☐ a member of an ineligible group.

- A group is ineligible if any of its members is:
  - ☐ a public company;
  - ☐ a corporate body whose shares are admitted to trading on a regulated market in an EEA State;
  - ☐ a person (other than a small company) authorised under FSMA 2000 to carry on a regulated activity;
  - ☐ a small company that is an authorised insurance company,

  s.384(2)

banking company, e-money issuer, MiFID investment firm or a UCITS management company; or
- ☐ a person who carries on insurance market activity.

Procedure

- The information required for abbreviated accounts of a small-sized company is:
  - ☐ full balance sheet;   s.444(1)
  - ☐ special auditors' report unless exempt from audit;   ss.449(2), (5)
  - ☐ abbreviated notes.
- Additionally there must be the following notes to the accounts:
  - ☐ A statement above the director's signature on the Balance   s.450(3)
    Sheet that the directors' accounts have relied on the exemptions for individual accounts, on the grounds that the company is entitled to benefit from those exemptions as a medium-sized company.

Filing requirement

Copy of the abbreviated accounts within the appropriate timescale,   s.442
usually six months for a public company or nine months for a private company (see page 5).

Notes

Copies of the full statutory accounts are still required to be circu-   s.423
lated to members within the appropriate timescale: six months for a public company and nine months for a private company.

More information

☐ Handbook: Chapter 10. 📖 Manual: Chapter 16.
(i) Companies House: GBA3.

Acquisition of non-cash assets from members in initial period

Special requirements apply where a public company proposes to acquire non-cash assets from its subscribers within the period of two years commencing on the date of the issue of its trading certificate, or in circumstances where a private company is re-registered as a public company and the company wishes to acquire certain non-cash assets from the members of the company, either at that time or within a period of two years from the re-registration.

s.598

s.603

In either circumstance the company may only acquire non-cash assets from its subscribers or members provided the assets are independently valued and approval is obtained from the members. These provisions do not apply where it is part of the company's ordinary business to acquire such assets and the transaction is entered into in the normal course of its business.

s.598(3)

s.603

s.598(4)

These provisions should not be confused with the provisions relating to the issue of shares for non-cash consideration, which are subject to s.593 (see page 202).

Checklist

- Is the asset being transferred from a subscriber or from a person who was a member at the date of re-registration as a public company?

  ss.598(1), 603(a)

- Is the value of the asset equal to 10 per cent or more of the companyissued share capital?

  s.598(1)(c)

- Is the transfer taking place within two years of issue of its s.761 trading certificate for transfers from a subscriber or within two years of re-registration as a public company in respect of transfers from a member?

  ss.598(2), 603(b)

- Appoint an independent valuer to value the asset being acquired in accordance with ss.1150 and 1153 and any non-cash consideration issued by the company (usually shares credited as fully paid).

  s.599
  s.600

- Valuation must be within six-month period prior to the date of transfer of the assets and must be circulated to members and the other party to the transfer.

  ss.599(1)

- Transfer agreement to be approved by members by ordinary resolution and a copy of the resolution must be forwarded to the other party to the transfer. s.601
- A copy of the ordinary resolution and the valuation report must be filed at Companies House within 15 days of the passing of the resolution. s.602

Procedure

- Convene a directors' meeting to appoint an independent valuer, usually the company's external accountant or auditors where appointed, recommend appropriate resolution(s) to members and to convene a general meeting. Ensure valid quorum present.
- A copy of the valuation report drawn up to a date not more than six months prior to the date of transfer must be received by the company. The valuation report must state those matters set out in s.600(2). s.599(1)(b)
- Issue notice, signed by director or company secretary, together with a copy of the valuation report convening the general meeting on 14 clear days' notice for members to consider resolution to approve transfer agreement and valuation report. ss.599(1)(c), 601(1)(a)
- Enclose with the notice a form of proxy if desired. Listed companies must enclose a two-way form of proxy (see page 176).
- Consider whether class meeting(s) also required.
- If the meeting is to be convened at short notice, the company secretary should arrange for agreement to short notice to be signed by each of the shareholders.
- Copy of valuation report and notice to be sent to the transferor of the assets if no longer a member. s.599(1)(c), 601(1)(c)
- Hold general meeting. Ensure valid quorum is present. Resolution put to vote either by show of hands or by poll and to be passed by appropriate majority (ordinary resolution by 50 per cent majority).

Filing requirement

- Signed copy of ordinary resolution and copy of the valuation report within 15 days of approval. s.602(1)

Notes

- The independent valuer's report must confirm that, in his or her opinion, the consideration to be received by the company is not less than the value of the consideration being paid (i.e. cash or shares).

- These provisions will apply even where the acquisition is only in part the acquisition of non-cash assets, provided that they exceed 10 per cent in nominal value of the company's issued share capital.
- Transactions involving assets with an aggregate value representing less than 10 per cent in nominal value of the company's issued share capital are exempt from these requirements.   s.598(1)(c)
- If these provisions have not been followed, the company is entitled to reclaim any consideration paid to its subscribers or members, in which case the agreement shall be void.   s.604
- If the consideration paid by the company is the allotment of shares credited as fully paid, the company shall be entitled to request from the allottee an amount equal to the nominal value of the shares together with any share premium.   s.604(3)

More information

Handbook: Chapter 5. Manual: Chapter 2.

Agreement to short notice

In most instances, members of private companies and small unquoted public companies can agree to accept shorter notice of a meeting than that prescribed by the Companies Act.

For any general meeting other than an annual general meeting of a public company, a majority of the members holding between them at least 90 per cent of the voting shares must agree to the meeting being held at short notice. This can be increased to not more than 95 per cent by a provision contained in the company's articles of association.

s.307(6)

For an annual general meeting of a public company, all members must agree.

s.337(2)

It is not necessary for the members agreeing to the short notice to attend the meeting.

It is recommended that the agreement(s) to short notice are given in writing and that these are placed in the company's minute book, together with the minutes of the meeting.

If the meeting is being convened by a public company to consider the company accounts, the agreement to short notice must include agreement to accept receipt of the accounts less than 21 days prior to the meeting being held, if these are being sent with the notice convening the meeting.

s.424(4)

Although certain resolutions require that special notice be given, calling the meeting on short notice will not in itself invalidate the resolution. However, caution must be taken when calling meetings on short notice of which special notice has been given.

Certain resolutions (e.g. purchase of own shares) require that documents be made available for inspection for a set period prior to the meeting. As a result, the option to convene the appropriate meeting on short notice is limited and for private companies using the written resolution procedure may be an appropriate alternative (see page 210).

Checklist

- In addition to the requisite percentage of the issued share capital, is a majority of the members represented?
- Do any documents need to be made available for inspection for a minimum period prior to the meeting?
- Confirm consent to short notice verbally, prior to issuing notice of meeting.

Procedure

- The company secretary to circulate an agreement to short notice with the notice and request its signature and return.

Filing requirement

- There are no filing requirements.

More information

Handbook: Chapter 9. Manual: Chapter 14.

Annual general meeting

Private companies do not need to hold an annual general meeting unless their articles of association require this. Where required to hold an annual general meeting by their articles of association, the notice period, in the absence of any provisions of the articles of association, is the same as for any general meeting.

A public company must hold an annual general meeting within six months of its accounting reference date. Where its accounting reference period is shortened, the annual general meeting must be held within three months of the giving of the notice to shorten the accounting period.

s.336(1)

s.336(2)

As a consequence, a public company may not need to hold an annual general meeting in any particular calendar year if it has a financial year in excess of 12 months.

The normal or 'ordinary' business of the AGM is to receive the most recent accounts, consideration of the remuneration report (quoted companies only) confirm the declaration of a final dividend (where appropriate), approve the remuneration of the auditors, and re-elect the auditors and retiring directors, if necessary. Any other business is deemed to be 'special' business.

Checklist

- The meeting must be held within six months of the company's accounting reference date.

  s.336(1)

- If the directors propose payment of a final dividend, this must be approved at a general meeting.

  art.70 Sch.3
  SI 2008/3229

- If the company is quoted, a resolution to approve the directors' remuneration report will be required.

  s.439

- Check the articles of association to see if the directors are required to retire by rotation.
- Check the articles of association to see if any new directors appointed by the directors during the year are required to retire at the annual general meeting. If the company is a public company, each director offering themselves for re-election will require a separate resolution.

  s.160

- Check the articles to see if there are any special requirements for the election or re-election of directors.
- Check to see if any members have validly proposed any resolutions required to be included in the notice (see page 210).   s.338
- Are the auditors to be re-appointed, or are new auditors being appointed requiring special notice (see page 37)?   ss.489, 515
- The remuneration of the auditors must be fixed by the members or in such manner as they shall approve.   s.492
- If appropriate, a resolution to extend or renew any authority (see page 224) to issue shares can be put as special business.   ss.549, 551
- If appropriate, a resolution to extend or renew any waiver of pre-emption rights on allotment (see page 169) can be put as special business.   ss.561, 570, 571, 573
- Consider whether there is any other business to be put before the members.

Procedure

- Convene a directors' meeting to recommend appropriate resolution(s) to members and to convene annual general meeting. Ensure valid quorum present.
- Company secretary or director to give special notice to the company, if required (such as appointment of auditors other than retiring auditors).   s.312
- Issue notice, signed by director or company secretary, convening annual general meeting of a public company on 21 clear days' notice (20 clear working days, for a quoted company) for members to consider resolutions. Private companies holding an annual general meeting need only give 14 clear days' notice, subject to the articles of association.   s.337 s.307
- Notice may be given by placing it on a website and notifying members where the notice may be viewed.   s.309
- Enclose with the notice a copy of any accounts and a form of proxy if desired. Where issued forms of proxy must be sent to all members entitled to vote at the meeting. Listed companies must enclose a three-way form of proxy (see page 176).   s.326 LR 9.3·6
- Consider whether class meeting(s) also required.
- If the meeting is to be convened on short notice, the company secretary should arrange for agreement to short notice to be signed by each of the members (see page 24).   s.502(2)
- Copy of notice to be sent to non-member directors and auditors.
- Hold annual general meeting. Ensure valid quorum is present. Resolutions put to vote either by show of hands or by poll and to be passed by appropriate majority (ordinary resolution by 50 per cent majority, special resolutions by 75 per cent majority).

Filing requirement

- Copies of any special resolutions and those ordinary resolutions   ss.29, 30
  where notification required.
- Any appropriate forms relating to non-reappointment of direc-   ss.167, 521
  tors or auditors.

Notes

- The company secretary should arrange a suitable venue for the
  meeting.
- Before the meeting, the company secretary, or if appointed
  the company's share registrars, should check and count all the
  proxies received.
- At the meeting, the company secretary should ensure that an
  attendance sheet is circulated.
- Arrangements should be made to ensure that shareholders alone
  have access to the meeting; however, this is not always possible
  or desirable in practice.
- Unless waived by the meeting, the notice and the directors'
  report should be read to the meeting.
- There is no longer a statutory requirement for the audit report to
  be read to the meeting. However, if the auditor is present, it is
  usual practice for him or her to read the audit opinion.
- For companies with a large number of shareholders, or at meetings where there may be questions from the floor, it is useful to
  prepare a chairman's script prior to the meeting. Additionally,
  the directors should meet before the meeting to discuss any
  matters that might be raised at the meeting and decide who will
  deal with certain queries.
- If a poll is likely, the company secretary should arrange for
  poll cards to be available. Companies who use registrars will
  normally use their services when conducting a poll. The directors
  should ensure that as many proxy forms as possible are received
  prior to the meeting. It is important that proxy forms are
  received at the registered office, or the office of the registrars, 48
  hours before the meeting. Proxy forms arriving later than this
  cannot be accepted, and any proxy forms brought to the meeting
  are invalid.
- Additional copies of the latest audited accounts and directors'
  service contracts must be available at the meeting, together
  with a copy of the Register of Members, minutes of previous
  shareholder meetings and the Registers of Directors, Directors'
  Interests and copies of directors' service contracts.

More information

Handbook: Chapter 9. Manual: Chapter 14.

Annual returns

All companies are required to file annual returns (Form AR01), made up to a date not more than 12 months from the date of the previous annual return, the return date.

s.854

The annual return must be filed within 28 days of its made-up date.

s.854(3)

Although annual returns will be accepted for filing outside the 28-day period, where the return has been made to a date prior to its existing return date, then this return date will remain unaltered. In such circumstances a second return will be due, made up to the return date.

Companies no longer receive a 'shuttle' form of annual return. Instead companies will receive a reminder letter from Companies House approximately one month prior to the due date. Companies can either request or download a blank annual return form from Companies House, or complete the form online using web filing (see page 68) or use proprietary software to file the form electronically.

The annual return provides a snapshot of the company's managers and members and contains details of its registered office, the type of company and its principal business activities, its directors, company secretary (where appointed), place of inspection of the register of members if not at the registered office, place of inspection of the register of debenture holders if not at the registered office, statement of capital and details of members.

ss,856, 857

Checklist

- Check or complete the annual return information as set out below.
- Provide details of any changes in shareholders and if there have been none, supply a complete list at least once every three years.
- File the annual return within 28 days of the made-up date, together with the appropriate filing fee: £30 if being filed in hard copy, and £15 if being filed electronically or online.

Procedure

- For all companies, the following information must be disclosed on the annual return for all companies: s.855
  - □ Name of the company, as registered.
  - □ Registered number.
  - □ Type of company.
  - □ Whether the company was a traded company at any time during the period covered by the annual return. A company is traded if its shares are listed by the UKLA.
  - □ Registered office address.
  - □ Address where any company records are kept if not at registered office.
  - □ Principal business activities of the company
  - □ Name and address of the company secretary, where appointed   s.856A
  - □ Name, service address, date of birth, nationality and business occupation of all directors.   s.856B
  - □ The date to which the annual return is made up.
- If the company has shares, a Statement of Capital and members particulars as follows:
  - □ Total number and aggregate nominal of shares in issue.
  - □ For each class of share, details of the voting rights attached to each class, total number and aggregate nominal value of shares in issue.
  - □ Amounts paid up and any unpaid amounts.
- If the company is not a traded company, the name of every member, their holding of shares at the return date, and details of any transfers by or to each person who was a member at any time during the period since the date of the previous annual return or date of incorporation in the case of a company's first annual return.
- If the company is a traded company, for every member who held 5 per cent or more of the issued shares at any time during the period covered by the return, their name, address and holding of shares at the return date and details of any transfers by or to each such member since the date of the previous annual return or date of incorporation in the case of a company's first annual return.

Filing requirement

- Annual return form AR01 within 28 days of made-up date.
- Filing fee: £30 or £15 as appropriate.

Notes

- Companies with large numbers of shareholders are encouraged to submit this information on floppy disc or CD-Rom.
- It is an offence not to deliver a company's annual return within 28 days of the made-up date, for which the company, company secretary where appointed, and directors may be prosecuted.

s.858

More information

Handbook: Chapter 14. Manual: Chapter 10.
Companies House: GBA2.

Articles of Association (adoption or change)

The articles of association are the rules governing the company's internal affairs. SI 2008/3229 contains model sets of articles, appropriate for private companies limited by shares, private companies limited by guarantee and public companies (see page 88).
s.20

Under all previous Companies Acts, default articles of association were contained in Table A to the particular Companies Act in force when the company was incorporated.

Companies incorporated prior to 1 October 2009 will have as their default articles the version of Table A in force when the company was incorporated, and later versions do not apply unless specifically adopted by a company.

The model articles apply to any particular company to the extent that they are not excluded or varied by the company's articles.
s.20(1)(b)

Alteration of any particular regulation or adoption of new articles requires a special resolution of the members in general meeting.
s.21

Articles may contain entrenched provisions. Amendment of entrenched provisions requires 100 per cent consent from members entitled to vote or a court order.
s.22

Checklist
- If the company has more than one class of shares, separate class meeting may also be required.
- Check whether rights to be amended are entrenched.
- Consider whether amendment can be undertaken by amending existing clauses, by the adoption of new clauses in addition to or in substitution for existing clauses or by the adoption of a complete new set of articles.

Procedure
- Convene a directors' meeting to recommend resolutions to members and to convene a general meeting or, in the case of a

private company, circulate a written resolution if appropriate (see page 210).

- Issue notice, signed by director or company secretary, convening general meeting on 14 clear days' notice, or circulate written resolution for members to consider special resolution to amend the articles.

s.21

- As a special resolution the resolution must contain the full text of the proposed changes.
- Consider whether a class meeting is also required.
- If the meeting is to be convened on short notice (see page 24), the company secretary should arrange for agreement to short notice to be signed by each of the shareholders.
- Hold general meeting. Ensure valid quorum is present. Resolutions put to vote either by show of hands or by poll and to be passed by appropriate majority (special resolution by 75 per cent majority)

s.283

- If the resolution is circulated by means of a written resolution the resolution must receive approval of the holders of at least 75 per cent of the members entitled to vote within 28 days of the circulation date of the resolution (see page 210).

Filing requirement

- Signed copy of special resolution within 15 days. ss.29(1)(a), 30(1)
- Amended copy of the articles of association with copy resolution. s.26

Notes

- Although it is not necessary to issue new copies of the articles of association to the shareholders, the company should ensure that it has a supply for issue to those shareholders who request a copy. In addition, a copy will normally be sent to the company's bankers and to their auditors.
- If a company files a copy of a resolution amending its articles but does not file a copy of the amended articles, Companies House may issue a notice requiring an amended copy of the articles be filed within a specified time. For failure to file the amended copy within the specified time, the company will a liable to a £200 fine.

s.27
s.27(4)

More information

Handbook: Chapter 1. Manual: Chapter 1.
Companies House: GBF1.

Auditors – appointment to private company

With the exception of private companies that are exempt from audit, dormant companies and non-profit-making companies subject to public sector audit, all companies must appoint auditors and prepare audited accounts.

s.475

The members of a company which is exempt from audit may require it to appoint auditors, provided this request is made by members holding at least 10 per cent in nominal value of its issued shares, or 10 per cent of the members, for a company without shares.

s.476

Directors will usually appoint auditors, where they are being appointed for the first time or following a period where an audit was not required.

Directors may appoint auditors at any time before the company's first or next period for appointing auditors (see below), or to fill a casual vacancy.

s.485(3)

If a company has no auditors, members may appoint auditors during a period for appointing auditors.

s.485(4)

The period for appointing auditors is the period of 28 days beginning on the end of the period for sending out the accounts to members for the previous financial year, or if earlier, the day the accounts for the previous financial year were sent out.

s.485(2)

If a company that is required to have its accounts audited fails to appoint auditors, notification of that must be sent to the Secretary of State and the Secretary of State may appoint auditors to fill the vacancy.

s.486

An auditor is required to be registered as an auditor, and must not be an officer or a servant of the company, or a partner or employee of such officers or servants. An auditor may be an individual, a partnership or a limited company.

ss.1211–1215

Checklist

- Does the company qualify for exemption from audit?   s.475
- Has an audit been requested by members?   s.476
- Is the person to be appointed eligible?   s.1211
    - ☐ Member of a recognised supervisory body.   s.1212
    - ☐ Not an officer or employee of the company or partner or employee of an officer or employee of the company.   s.1214
    - ☐ Not connected with the company or an associated undertaking.   s.1215

Procedure

- Convene a directors' meeting to consider the appointment of auditors. Ensure valid quorum present.
- Where the appointment is to be by the members, this is by an ordinary resolution, either at a general meeting convened by the directors or by written resolution of the members.
- A company that has no auditors may have auditors appointed by the Secretary of State.

Filing requirement

- The appointment of auditors does not need to be notified to Companies House

Notes

- The company may wish to notify its bankers, solicitors, subsidiaries, etc, of the auditors' appointment

More information

Handbook: Chapter 11. Manual: Chapter 15.
Companies House: GBA4.

Auditors – appointment to public company

With the exception of dormant public companies that are exempt from audit, all public companies must appoint auditors and prepare audited accounts.

s.489(1)

Directors may appoint auditors at any time before the company's first general meeting to receive audited accounts or to fill a casual vacancy.

s.489(3))

Members may appoint auditors, by ordinary resolution, at a general meeting at which audited accounts have been laid or in circumstances when the company should have had auditors appointed but does not have auditors.

s.489(4)

If a public company that is required to have its accounts audited fails to appoint auditors notification of that must be sent to the Secretary of State and the Secretary of State may appoint auditors to fill the vacancy.

s.490

An auditor is required to be registered as an auditor, and must not be an officer or a servant of the company, or a partner or employee of such officers or servants. An auditor may be an individual, a partnership or a limited company.

ss.1211~1215

Checklist

- Does the company qualify for exemption from audit?   s.475
- Is the person to be appointed eligible?   s.1211
  - Member of a recognised supervisory body.   s.1212
  - Not an officer or employee of the company or partner or employee of an officer or employee of the company.   s.1214
  - Not connected with the company or an associated undertaking.   s.1215

Procedure

- Convene a directors' meeting to consider the appointment of auditors. Ensure valid quorum present.

- Where the appointment is to be by the members, this is by an ordinary resolution either at a general meeting convened by the directors or by written resolution of the members.
- A public company that has no auditors may have auditors appointed by the Secretary of State.
- Auditors of a public company are appointed to hold office only until the conclusion of the next general meeting at which accounts are laid before the members, when they may be re-appointed.

s.491

Filing requirement

- The appointment of auditors does not need to be notified to Companies House.

Notes

- The company may wish to notify its bankers, solicitors, subsidiaries, etc. of the auditors' appointment.

More information

Handbook: Chapter 11. Manual: Chapter 15.
Companies House: GBA4.

Auditors – removal

The members of a company may remove the auditors from office by ordinary resolution. In practice, the directors will normally invite the auditors to resign, or will propose that the auditors are not re-appointed at a general meeting at which accounts are to be laid.

s.510

Checklist

- Special notice must be given to the company of a proposed resolution to remove auditors.
- A copy of the special notice must be sent to the auditors whose removal is proposed.
- The auditors may make a written representation concerning their removal and request its notification to the members either by post or if there is insufficient time by reading it to the meeting.
- The auditors' representation need not be notified to members if an application to the court it is upheld.
- On removal, notice of that removal must be filed at Companies House within 14 days.

s.511

s.511(2)

s.511(3)

s.511(6)

s.512

Procedure

- Special notice given by a director to the company.
- Convene a directors' meeting to recommend resolution to members and to convene a general meeting. Ensure valid quorum present.
- Copy of the special notice sent to the auditors.
- Issue notice, signed by director or company secretary, convening general meeting with 14 clear days' notice for members to consider :
  - ☐ ordinary resolution to remove auditors;
  - ☐ whether a class meeting is also required.
- If the meeting is to be convened on short notice, the company secretary should arrange for agreement to short notice to be signed by each of the shareholders.
- Representation of auditors circulated with notice, or separately.

- If appropriate, seek court order that representation need not be circulated or read out at meeting.
- If not circulated and no court order obtained, read auditors' representation to meeting.
- Hold general meeting. Ensure valid quorum is present. Resolutions put to vote either by show of hands or by poll and to be passed by appropriate majority (ordinary resolution by 50 per cent majority).
- Notify auditors of result of meeting.
- If removal approved, notify Companies House.

Filing requirement

- Form AA03 within 14 days.

Notes

- If a shareholder gives notice of their intention to propose the removal of the auditors, unless they also requisition a general meeting there is no requirement for the directors to convene a meeting. The resolution would however be required to be put at the next general meeting.
- The written resolution procedure cannot be used and the resolution must be put to a general meeting of the members.

More information

Handbook: Chapter 11. Manual: Chapter 15.
 Companies House: GBA4.

Auditors – resignation

Auditors may resign from office by giving notice in writing to the registered office of the company. To be effective, the notice of resignation must be accompanied by a statement of any matters that they consider should be brought to the attention of members, or if there are no such circumstances, a statement to that effect.

s.516

s.516(2)

s.519

Checklist

- Auditors' resignation and s.519 statement received at the registered office.
- Copy of resignation letter to be filed at Companies House by the company within 14 days.
- If there are circumstances to be notified to the members or creditors, the statement must be circulated to members within 14 days, or apply to the court for an order that it need not do so.
- If court order sought, notify auditors.
- Unless notice of application for court order received within 21 days, the auditors to file a copy of their statement with Companies House within 28 days of original notice of resignation.
- If court order not obtained, the company must circulate the statement to members within 14 days of the court's decision and notify the auditors, who shall file a copy of their statement at Companies House within the next seven days.

s.517

s.520

s.520(3)
s.521

ss.520(5),
521(2)

Procedure

- File copy of auditors' resignation at Companies House provided statement of circumstances also received.
- Circulate statement of circumstances, if any, to members, or apply to court for order not to circulate. If court order sought, notify auditors within 21 days of original notice being received.

Filing requirement

- Copy of auditors' resignation letter within 14 days.
- Auditors to file statement of circumstances after 21 days, but before 28 days, unless application to court made.

- If court uphold application, copy of that decision to be circulated to members.
- If application not upheld, statement to be circulated to members within 14 days, and notifying auditors who must file their statement at Companies House within the next seven days.

More information

Handbook: Chapter 11. Manual: Chapter 15.
Companies House: GBA4.

Bank account

The company's bank account and banking matters generally are controlled by the board of directors.

All banks have a standard form of mandate, and this is usually presented as a draft minute. Once the text of the authority and the instructions have been approved by the directors, a copy of the signed mandate should be inserted in the company's minute book as evidence of the appropriate decisions having been reached.

The majority of banks require security or collateral for overdraft facilities, and care must be taken to ensure that the directors have authority to charge the company's assets.

Checklist

- Completed bank mandate form.
- Approved by the directors.
- Originals or certified copies of memorandum and articles of association, certificate of incorporation and any changes of name certificate to commence trading (public companies only).
- Money laundering verification of identity documents as advised by the bank. Often original or certified copies of passport or driving licence and a utility bill showing residential address will suffice.

Procedure

Convene a directors' meeting to consider the terms of the bank mandate and approve the opening of the account. Ensure valid quorum present.

Filing requirement

- None

Notes

- The bank will note and return the original certificates of incorporation and any change of name certificates.
- Care must be taken to ensure that the signatories required for cheques are reasonable in the circumstances. Many companies empower an authorised signatory to sign cheques up to a certain limit, with directors (often two) required to sign cheques of larger amounts.
- The frequency with which the company is to receive bank statements should also be agreed.
- The banks prefer the mandate to be expressed in terms of the position held by the signatories rather than their names. If a named person is shown, when that person leaves the company it is necessary to complete a new mandate, rather than merely change the signatory.
- It is normal practice to inform the bank whenever there are changes to the company's directors, company secretary, registered office, the company's accounting reference date or the company's auditors.
- The bank will often require a copy of the company's latest audited accounts for their records.

More information

Handbook: Chapter 7. Manual: Chapter 7.

Bearer shares

A company, if authorised by its articles of association, may issue a share warrant, in respect of any of its fully paid shares, the bearer of which is entitled to the shares specified in the warrant. These shares are commonly referred to as bearer shares.

s.779

Share warrants can be issued in respect of fully paid shares either upon allotment or transfer of shares. As there is no instrument of transfer for a share warrant, transfer being effected by physical transfer of the share warrant itself, stamp duty is payable on the issue of the warrant and not on the transfer of a warrant.

s.779(1)

Checklist

- Check that the articles of association permit the issue of share warrants. This authority is not contained in the model articles for private companies but is contained in the model articles for public companies.

reg. 51 Sch.3
SI 2008/3229

Procedure to transfer

- The member should make a request in writing for their shares to be converted into bearer form and lodge this request and their share certificate(s) with the company.
- Using forms B1 1 and B1 2, available from stamp offices, the appropriate stamp duty, currently 1.5 per cent, is payable on the issue of share warrants. The duty is payable by the member whose shares are being converted to bearer form.
- Convene a directors' meeting to approve the issue of a share warrant in place of the shares. Ensure valid quorum present.
- The share warrant document should be collected or delivered to the shareholder and a confirmation of receipt obtained.
- The register of members will require updating.

Filing requirement

- None.

Notes

- As the holders of share warrants will not be known to the company, and their details are not registered with the company when meetings are convened, newspaper advertisements to notify holders of warrants are also required.
- If dividends are to be paid, arrangements will be required by which holders of warrants can claim their dividend by attending in person with their share warrant as proof of entitlement.
- Share warrants can be returned to the company and the shares represented on the warrant registered in the name of the person lodging the warrant.

More information

Handbook: Chapter 4. Manual: Chapter 5.

Bonus issue (capitalisation issue)

A bonus or capitalisation issue is the means by which the company allots shares that are partly or fully paid, by capitalising reserves. No further payment from the shareholder is normally required. If the bonus shares are partly paid, the unpaid portion may be called at some future date.

The company's capacity to issue partly or fully paid shares is included in the model articles for a private and public companies, but also requires approval of the shareholders by ordinary resolution. Although a bonus issue is an issue of new shares, no new capital is raised; it is effected by capitalising some or all of the company's distributable reserves.

Sch.1 reg.36,
Sch.3 reg.78
SI 2008/3229

Companies may wish to issue shares in this manner for a number of reasons. These include:

- to increase the company's issued share capital in order to meet the minimum capital requirement when re-registering as a public company without requiring the shareholders to inject further funds (see page 202);
- to declare a bonus issue in conjunction with a rights issue to reduce the potential dilution of the holdings of those shareholders who do not take up any shares under the offer; or
- to create a more substantial balance sheet by capitalising reserves into issued share capital.

Checklist

- Check the articles of association to ensure the issue of bonus shares is permitted, and if any procedures have been stipulated.
- Check the articles to ensure there are sufficient unissued shares available for issue.
- Check the articles of association to ensure the directors have authority in terms of s.551 to issue shares. If not, a resolution to extend or renew the authority will be required (see page 208).

Procedure

- Convene a directors' meeting to recommend appropriate resolution(s) to members and to convene a general meeting. Ensure valid quorum present.
- Issue notice, signed by director or company secretary, together convening the general meeting on 14 clear days' notice for members to consider resolution. Alternatively, a private company may circulate the resolutions by written resolution. ss.281, 307
- Enclose with the notice a form of proxy if desired. Listed companies must enclose a three-way form of proxy (see page 176).
- Consider whether class meeting(s) also required.
- If the meeting is to be convened on short notice, the company secretary should arrange for agreement to short notice to be signed by the appropriate number of the shareholders (see page 23). s.307(5)
- Copy of notice to be sent to non-member directors and auditors. ss.310, 502
- Hold general meeting. Ensure valid quorum is present. Resolution put to vote either by show of hands or by poll and to be passed by appropriate majority (ordinary resolution by 50 per cent majority).
- Following meeting, issue new share certificates and update register of members. If there is to be a delay before share certificates are issued, it may be appropriate to issue allotment letters giving details of each member's entitlement to new shares. In any event, new share certificates must be issued within two months. s.554 / s.769

Filing requirement

- Form SH01 within one month. s.555
- Statement of capital. s.555

Notes

- As bonus shares are issued *pro rata*, it should not be necessary to waive any rights of pre-emption, unless the members have the option to renounce their entitlement.
- On completion of the bonus issue, the company's accountants, both internal and external, must be informed, so that the appropriate entries to the company's accounts can be made.
- If it is necessary to increase or renew s.551 authority to issue shares (see page 169), there will be additional filing requirements.

More information

Handbook: Chapter 5. Manual: Chapter 3.

Borrowing powers

All companies are deemed to have full capacity unless the articles place specific restrictions on the company.

The articles of listed companies will often restrict the directors' ability to exercise the full borrowing powers of the company. The limitation is often expressed as a multiple of the company's net assets, and so will vary over time.

Directors of companies incorporated under previous Companies Acts have only the restricted borrowing power contained in the articles, unless this authority contained in the 'old' Table A has been amended in the articles or by subsequent resolution (see page 50).

If the directors' capacity to exercise the company's borrowing power is not sufficient for their purposes, the articles of association will need to be amended by special resolution (see page 32).

Checklist

- Check the articles of association for any restriction of either the company's capacity to borrow or the directors' authority to exercise that borrowing capacity.

More information

Handbook: Chapter 2. Manual: Chapter 9.

Business names

A business name is a name or title by which a company may trade, other than its corporate or registered name.

There is no longer a register of business names.

The business stationery of a company using a business name must show the company name in full as well as the business name, in addition to the other statutory requirements (see page 112).

reg.6 SI 2008/495

The name of the proprietor must be shown at all business premises.

reg.4 SI 2008/495

Companies using business names must ensure they do not infringe registered names or trade marks, or pass themselves off as other registered companies, partnerships or sole traders.

Checklist

- Is the company's registered name shown on all headed paper, invoices, cheques etc.
- Is the company's registered name displayed outside all business premises
- Is the fact that the company is the proprietor of the business displayed at all business premises.

Filing requirement

- None.

More information

Handbook: Chapter 1. Manual: Chapter 1.

Calls

Where, for any reason, shares have been issued as partly or nil paid, the amounts unpaid can be called by the directors at any time, either in full or in part.

The liability for the unpaid amounts rests with the registered holder.

The company should not accept registration of a transfer of shares on which there remains an unpaid call, unless the transferee is willing to pay the unpaid call.

The model articles for private companies do not permit partly or nil paid shares to be issued, and accordingly if such shares are to be issued, the articles will require amendment. Table A to the Companies Act 1985 provided for partly paid shares and contained provisions for the making of calls by directors. The model articles for public companies contain provisions for the making of calls on partly paid shares.

art.21 Sch.1 SI 2008/3229

arts 54-61 Sch.3 SI 2008/3229

Checklist

- Check the articles of association for the procedure to follow where a call is proposed. The procedure below follows the model wording for public companies.

Procedure

- Convene a directors' meeting to approve the making of a call.
- The company secretary should arrange the preparation and issue of call notices to members. Each call notice should be addressed to the registered holder or joint holders, as the case may be, and should contain details of the registered member(s), the amounts currently outstanding and the amount now being called, together with details of where and when the payment is due, which must be at least 14 days after the date of the call notice.
- Each call notice should carry a distinguishing number, and this number should be noted on the register of members, together

with a note of the amount being called. The company should compile lists of the payments as they are received and cleared by the bank. Once the date on which the call is due has passed, the list of payments should be reconciled with the register of members and a list of unpaid calls should be prepared.

- A reminder letter should be sent to all members that have not paid the call, requesting immediate payment and warning of the potential penalties for non-payment, including forfeiture of shares (see page 107) or suspension of voting rights.
- Members should return their share certificates together with a copy of the call notice so that the company can endorse the share certificates, giving details of the paid call. The endorsed share certificate should be returned to the shareholder. Alternatively the share certificates can be cancelled and new, fully paid, share certificates issued.
- The Register of Members should be amended to include details of the additional amounts now paid on the shares.
- If a call remains unpaid interest is due at a rate to be set by the directors but not to exceed 5 per cent above the base lending rate in force from time to time. Directors may waive the obligation to pay interest either in part or in full.

Filing requirement

- None.

Notes

- Where calls remain unpaid, a number of actions can be taken, although the articles of association should be checked to ensure that the directors have the requisite authority.
- The directors may institute proceedings for the forfeiture of the shares, under which circumstance the shares are forfeited by the holder, and cancelled or reissued. In the instance of reissue, the company should return to the shareholders the amounts paid by them on the shares. The articles of association may authorise the directors to withhold any dividends from the shareholder, and credit these amounts to the share capital account until such time as the call has been paid.
- Alternatively, the shareholder may lose the right to vote until such time as the call has been paid.
- It will be necessary to inform the company's auditors of the call and the split between the calls that were paid and any unpaid calls. Occasionally, shares will be issued as partly paid, with the balance payable on fixed instalment dates. The procedure to be

followed in such circumstances is the same as that for making a call.

More information

Handbook: Chapter 5. Manual: Chapter 2.
Companies House: GBA6.

Certification of shares

When members are transferring only part of their holding, they may be unwilling to forward their share certificate to the purchaser. In such circumstances the transferor should forward the certificate and stock transfer form to the company or its registrar, for certifying. The company or its registrar will then stamp the transfer form, stating that the certificate representing the shares on the transfer form has been lodged with the company/registrar and will return a balance certificate to the transferor if appropriate.

Certifications are most commonly used by stockbrokers and market-makers in respect of partial sales for quoted shares. These, however, are becoming less used following the introduction of the paperless settlement system, CREST.

Checklist

- Check the register of members to confirm that the share certificate has not previously been cancelled and is valid.
- Check that the transferors details on the transfer from match the holder shown on the share certificate, and that the transfer form is signed by the transferor.

Procedure

- Cancel the share certificate and insert on the transfer form reference details for the certification.
- Update the register of members to record the certification details and the cancellation of the original share certificate.
- Return the now certified transfer form to the person lodging it.

Filing requirement

- None.

More information

Handbook: Chapter 8. Manual: Chapter 5.

Combined code

The Combined Code is a guide to best practice which listed companies should either comply with or explain any departures from best practice.

The Combined Code was first issued in 1998 and has been updated regularly. At present, two versions are in effect: the 2006 edition and the June 2008 edition which applies to applies to accounting periods beginning on or after 29 June 2008.

Compliance with the Combined Code is not intended to be an exercise in 'box ticking', and compliance with certain aspects of the code may not be appropriate for all companies.

This checklist is intended to assist company secretaries monitoring their company's compliance with or explanations for any departure from the Combined Code (2008 version). The full Code should be referred to for details on any particular aspect.

Checklist	Code provision

Directors

The board:

■ Board to meet regularly.	A1.1
■ Formal schedule of matters reserved for the board.	A1.1
■ Statement in annual report of how the board operates and which types of decisions are reserved for the board or delegated to management.	A1.1
■ The annual report should identify the:	
□ chairman;	A1.2
□ deputy chairman – if any;	A1.2
□ chief executive;	A1.2
□ senior independent director;	A1.2
□ Independent non-executive directors	A3.1
□ chairmen and members of the board committees.	A1.2
■ Disclose number of meetings and attendance by directors.	A1.2
■ Chairman and non-executive directors to meet without the executives present.	A1.3

- Non-executive directors meet at least annually to appraise the chairman's performance.   A1.3
- Directors have concerns recorded in the board minutes.   A1.4
- Non-executive directors to provide a statement of concerns, if any, to chairman, for circulation to the board, on resignation.   A1.4
- Directors' insurance cover.   A1.5

Chairman and chief executive:

- Roles of chairman and chief executive separated.   A2.1
- Responsibilities between chairman and chief executive set out in writing.   A2.1
- Chairman to meet independence criteria at time of appointment. A2.2
- Chief executive not to become chairman.   A2.2
- If chief executive does become chairman, consult major shareholders and justify at time and in next annual report.   A2.2

Board balance and independence:

- Justify independence of non-executive directors if combined code criteria not met.   A3.1, A7.2, B1.3
- At least half the board, excluding the chairman, should be independent.   A3.2
- Small company to have at least two independent non-executive directors.   A3.2
- Appoint senior independent director.   A3.3
- Senior independent director to be available to meet shareholders. A3.3

Appointments to the board:

- Nomination committee leads process for board appointments.   A4.1
- Majority of the nomination committee to be independent non-executive directors.   A4.1
- Chairman or an independent non-executive director to chair the nomination committee.   A4.1
- Chairman should not chair the nomination committee when it is considering a successor to the chairman.   A4.1
- Nomination committee terms of reference, role and authority to be made available.   A4.1
- Role and capabilities for new directors to be assessed by the committee and a description prepared.   A4.2
- Job specification for chairman to be prepared by nomination committee.   A4.3
- Chairman's other commitments disclosed to the board prior to appointment and in annual report.   A4.3

- Changes to the chairman's other commitments reported and impact explained as they arise and in annual report.   A4.3
- Terms of appointment of non-executive directors to be available for inspection.   A4.4
- Non-executive director appointment letters should set out expected time commitment which each director should undertake that they can fulfil.   A4.4
- Non-executive directors other commitments to be disclosed to the board and informed of any changes.   A4.4
- Full-time executive directors should not have more than one non-executive directorship in a FTSE 100 company and not be chairman of such a company.   A4.5
- Work of the nomination committee to be described in annual report.   A4.6
- Justify in annual report if neither a search consultancy nor open advertising used in recruiting chairman or a non-executive director.   A4.6

Information and professional development:

- New directors should receive appropriate induction.   A5.1
- Major shareholders should have the opportunity to meet new non-executive directors.   A5.1
- Directors have access to independent professional advice.   A5.2
- Committees to be provided with sufficient resources to undertake their duties.   A5.2
- Directors have access to the company secretary.   A5.3
- Appointment and removal of company secretary matter for the board as a whole.   A5.3

Performance evaluation:

- Evaluation of the board, committees and directors detailed in annual report.   A6.1
- Non-executive directors responsible for evaluation of the chairman, taking into account the views of the executive directors.   A6.1

Re-election:

- Directors subject to election at the first AGM after their appointment.   A7.1
- Directors subject to re-election at least every three years.   A7.1
- Biographical details and other relevant information for directors subject to election or re-election to be provided to enable members to make an informed decision.   A7.1

- Non-executive directors appointed for specified terms (usually three years).   A7.2
- On proposed re-election, chairman to confirm that following a formal evaluation process the directors' continue to be effective.   A7.2
- Re-election of non-executive director after six years' service subject to rigorous review, and should take into account the need for progressive refreshing of the board.   A7.2
- Non-executive directors serving longer than nine years to be subject to annual re-election and may prejudice independence.   A7.2, A3.1

The level and make-up of remuneration:

- Performance-related pay should form a significant proportion of total pay of executive directors.   B1.1
- Remuneration package should align their interests with shareholders to give incentive.   B1.1
- Performance-related pay schemes should follow Sch.A of the Code.   B1.1
- No discounted share options save as permitted by Listing Rules.   B1.2
- Remuneration of non-executive directors reflects their time commitment and responsibilities.   B1.3
- Remuneration for non-executive directors should not include share options.   B1.3
- Shareholder approval sought if options are to be granted to non-executive directors and may prejudice independence criteria.   B1.3, A3.1
- Shares acquired on exercise of options to be held for at least one year after the non-executive director leaves the board.   B1.3
- If executive director(s) serve as non-executive directors for other companies details should be disclosed in the remuneration report of any pay received by the director.   B1.4

Remuneration

Service contracts and compensation

- Remuneration committee to consider compensation payments in the event of early termination so as to avoid payments to reward failure.   B1.5
- Compensation payments to reflect directors' obligations to mitigate loss.   B1.5
- Notice or contract periods to be one year or less.   B1.6
- If longer notice or contract periods for new directors, these should reduce to one year or less after the initial period.   B1.6

Procedure

- Remuneration committee to be at least three independent non-executive directors, two for smaller companies.   B2.1
- Chairman may be a member of the nomination committee, but not chair, provide they met the independence criteria on appointment (as chairman).   B2.1
- Remuneration committee terms of reference, role and authority to be made available.   B2.1
- If remuneration consultants are employed, details of any other connection with the company.   B2.1
- Remuneration committee to have delegated responsibility for setting remuneration of executive directors and the chairman including pension and any compensation payments.   B2.2
- The committee to recommend and monitor senior management remuneration and remuneration structure.   B2.2
- The board or, if required by the articles of association, the members, should determine non-executive director remuneration.   B2.3
- If permitted, the board may delegate this to a committee, which may include the chief executive.   B2.3
- Members' approval to be sought for all long-term incentive schemes and changes to existing schemes, except as permitted by the Listing Rules.   B2.4

Accountability and audit

Financial reporting

- Explanation in the annual report of directors' responsibility for preparing the accounts.   C1.1
- Statement in annual report by the auditors about their reporting responsibilities.   C1.1
- Directors should report that the business is a going concern, with assumptions or justification as necessary.   C1.2

Internal control

- The board should review, at least annually, the effectiveness of group's internal controls, and report to shareholders that they have done so.   C2.1 DTR 7.2.5
- The review to cover all material controls and risk management systems.   C2.1

Audit committee and auditors

- Audit committee to comprise at least three independent non-executive directors, two for smaller companies.   C3.1

- Chairman may be a member of the audit committee, but not chair, provided they met the independence criteria on appointment (as chairman). C3.1
- At least one audit committee member to have recent and relevant financial experience. C3.1
- Remuneration committee terms of reference, role and authority to be made available and cover at least:
  - ☐ monitor integrity of financial statements and formal announcements;
  - ☐ review internal financial controls and unless reserved for the board or a separate committee to review the internal control and risk management systems;
  - ☐ review internal audit function;
  - ☐ make recommendations to the board for the appointment, re-appointment, removal and to approve remuneration and terms of engagement of the external auditors;
  - ☐ review independence, objectivity and effectiveness of external auditors; and
  - ☐ develop and implement policy relating to use of the service of external auditors for non-audit services. C3.2, C3.3
- Annual report should describe the work of the committee in carrying out its duties. C3.3
- Audit committee to review arrangements for employees to raise concerns about possible improprieties. C3.4
- Audit committee's objective to ensure arrangements are in place for proportionate and independent investigation and for appropriate follow-up action. C3.4
- Audit committee to monitor and review the internal audit activities. C3.5
- Audit committee should consider annually whether there is a need for an internal audit function. C3.5
- Explain lack of internal audit function in the annual report. C3.5
- Audit committee to be responsible for recommending the appointment, reappointment and removal of the external auditors. C3.6
- If audit committee's recommendation not accepted, explain different position taken by board in annual report. C3.6
- Explain in annual report how auditors' objectivity and independence is safeguarded if auditors' provide non-audit services C3.7

Relations with shareholders

Dialogue with institutional shareholders

- Chairman to ensure views of shareholders are relayed to the board. D1.1

- Chairman to discuss governance and strategy with major shareholders.   D1.1
- Non-executive directors should have the opportunity to meet major shareholders and should expect to meet them if requested.   D1.1
- Senior independent director to meet with major shareholders to help develop an understanding of the issues and concerns of major shareholders.   D1.1
- Explain in annual report steps taken to ensure that the directors, and in particular the non-executive directors, understand the views of major shareholders.   D1.2

Constructive use of the AGM

- Separate resolution(s) for each substantially separate issue.   D2.1
- Propose a resolution relating to the report and accounts.   D2.1
- Proxy appointment forms should allow members to instruct their proxy to vote for or against resolutions, or to withhold their vote.   D2.1
- Proxy form and any declaration of the results of a vote to make it clear that a vote withheld is not a vote, and will not be included in calculating the proportion of votes for or against the resolution.   D2.1
- Unless a poll is called, indicate the level of proxy votes lodged on each resolution, after it has been dealt with on a show of hands   D2.2
- Ensure that proxy votes cast are properly received and recorded.   D2.2
- The chairmen of the board committees to be available to answer questions at the AGM.   D2.3
- All directors attend annual general meetings.   D2.3
- Notice of the AGM and related papers to be issued at least 20 working days before the meeting.   D2.4

More information

Handbook: Chapter 18. Manual: Chapter 12.

www.frc.org.uk.

Combined Code – annual report disclosures

The Combined Code is a guide to best practice; listed companies should either comply with the Code or explain any departures.

Additionally, specific reporting on certain aspects of the company's policies is required.

Checklist

Code provision

This checklist is intended to assist company secretaries in complying with the specific reporting requirements. The full Code should be referred to for details on any particular aspect.

	Code provision
■ Statement in annual report of how the board operates and which types of decisions are reserved for the board or delegated to management.	A1.1
■ The annual report should identify the:	
□ chairman;	A1.2
□ deputy chairman – if any;	A1.2
□ chief executive;	A1.2
□ senior independent director;	A1.2
□ independent non-executive directors;	A3.1
□ chairmen and members of the board committees.	A1.2
■ Disclose number of meetings and attendance by directors.	A1.2
■ If chief executive does become chairman, consult major shareholders and justify at time and in next annual report.	A2.2
■ Chairman's other commitments disclosed to the board prior to appointment and in annual report.	A4.3
■ Changes to the chairman's other commitments reported and impact explained as they arise and in annual report.	A4.3
■ Work of the nomination committee to be described in annual report.	A4.6
■ Justify in annual report if neither a search consultancy nor open advertising used in recruiting chairman or a non-executive director.	A4.6
■ Evaluation of the board, committees and directors detailed in annual report.	A6.1

- Biographical details and other relevant information for directors subject to election or re-election to be provided to enable members to make an informed decision.   A7.1

- On proposed re-election, chairman to confirm that following a formal evaluation process the directors continue to be effective.   A7.2

- Shareholder approval sought if options are to be granted to non-executive directors and may prejudice independence criteria.   B1.3, A3.1

- If executive director(s) serve as non-executive directors for other companies details should be disclosed in the remuneration report of any pay received by the director.   B1.4

- Members' approval to be sought for all long-term incentive schemes and changes to existing schemes, except as permitted by the Listing Rules.   B2.4

- Explanation in the annual report of directors' responsibility for preparing the accounts.   C1.1

- Statement in annual report by the auditors about their reporting responsibilities.   C1.1

- Directors should report that the business is a going concern, with assumptions or justification as necessary.   C1.2

- The board should review, at least annually, the effectiveness of group's internal controls, and report to shareholders that they have done so.   C2.1 / DTR 7.2.5

- Annual report should describe the work of the committee in carrying out its duties.   C3.3

- Explain any lack of internal audit function in the annual report.   C3.5

- If audit committee's recommendation not accepted, explain different position taken by board in annual report.   C3.6

- Explain in annual report how auditor objectivity and independence is safeguarded if auditors provide non-audit services.   C3.7

- Explain in annual report steps taken to ensure that the directors, and in particular the non-executive directors, understand the views of major shareholders.   D1.2

- Separate resolution(s) for each substantially separate issue.   D2.1

- Propose a resolution relating to the report and accounts.   D2.1

Companies House – addresses of offices

England and Wales
Companies House
Crown Way
Maindy
Cardiff
CF14 3UZ
DX 33050 Cardiff 1

Contact Centre. +44 (0)303 1234 5000
Lines open Monday to Friday 8.30 am–6.00 pm

http//www.companies-house.gov.uk/
Email. enquiries@companies-house.gov.uk

London Information Centre
21 Bloomsbury Street
London
WC1B 3XD

Contact Centre. +44 (0)303 1234 5000
Fax. +44 (0)20 7637 210

Scotland
Companies House
37 Castle Street
Edinburgh
EH1 2EB

Contact Centre. +44 (0)303 1234 5000

Northern Ireland
Companies Registry
1st Floor, Waterfront Plaza
8 Laganbank Road
Belfast
BT1 3BS

Contact Centre. +44 (0)84 5604 8888
Office Hours Monday to Friday 10.00 am–4.00 pm

More information

Companies website for directions and maps

www.companieshouse.gov.uk (England, Wales and Scotland)

www.detini.gov.uk follow Companies Registry link
(Northern Ireland)

Companies House – charges

The fees charged by Companies House in force as at 30 June 2009 for incorporation and registration services are:

Service	England, Wales and Scotland	Northern Ireland
Incorporation fee	£20	£35
Electronic incorporation fee	£15	–
Same-day incorporation fee	£50	–
Change of name fee	£10	£40
Same-day change of name fee	£50	–
Re-registration fee	£20	£35
Same day re-registration fee	£50	–
Same day simultaneous – re-registration and change of name fee	£100	–
Annual return sent on paper	£30	£20
Annual return sent electronically	£15	–
Overseas company registration fee	£20	–
Overseas company change of name fee	£10	–
Overseas company filing accounts fee	£30	£20
Registration of mortgage	£13	£25
Voluntary dissolution fee	£10	£10
Certified copies and certificates of fact		
Certified copy document	£15	£5
Certified copy certificate – same-day service	£50	–
Certificate of fact	£15	£5
Certificate of fact – same-day service	£50	–

More information

Full price list available from Companies House website

www.companieshouse.gov.uk/toolsToHelp/productListcompare.shtml

www.detini.gov.uk

Companies House – electronic filing

Electronic filing is only available using an approved software package. At present there are about 20 suppliers of software for the forms and about 35 suppliers offering electronic incorporation software. A full list and contact information for these suppliers can be found on the Companies House website (www.companies house. gov.uk/toolsToHelp/efSoftwareSupp.shtml).

Checklist

- Proprietary software.
- Registration with Companies House.

Procedure

- Presenters must first register with Companies House. As part of this process an account will be opened for the payment of any filing fees.
- The company must notify Companies House of a password to authenticate documents and of the presenter transmitting the documents. This password will replace the signature of the company secretary or a director currently required to authenticate all forms.
- Groups of companies can choose to have the same password. In order to comply with the Companies Act, the password must be delivered to Companies House in writing by the company, and signed by a serving officer of the company.
- When a form detailing the appointment of a director or company secretary is delivered, the appointee is required to indicate his or her consent to act as a director or company secretary by providing three pieces of information which other people would not normally be expected to know. This information will not be displayed on the public file, but will be stored so that it can be retrieved should any question arise as to the validity of the appointment. Such personal information includes place of birth, mother's maiden name, NI number, passport number etc.

Alternatively a director or company secretary may agree with Companies House a six-digit personal identification code.

More information

Handbook: Chapter 14. Manual: Chapter 10.
Companies House: http://www.companieshouse.gov.uk/
    toolsToHelp/efiling.shtml .

Companies House – web filing

Companies House (not Northern Ireland) has introduced an electronic web filing service, currently limited to the most popular forms, with more forms becoming available according to demand. Currently the following forms may be filed using the web filing service:

Annual return	AR01
Change of accounting reference date	AA01
Appointment of director	AP01
Appointment of secretary	AP03
Termination of appointment of director	TM01
Termination of appointment of secretary	TM02
Change of director's details	CH01
Change secretary's details	CH03
Change of registered office address	AD01
Notification of single alternative inspection location	AD02
Return of allotment of shares	SH01
Dormant company accounts	AA02

Checklist

- Registration with Companies House.

Procedure

- Presenters must first register with Companies House. As part of this process an account will be opened for the payment of any filing fees.
- The company must notify Companies House of a password to authenticate documents and of the presenter transmitting the documents. This password will replace the signature of the secretary or a director currently required to authenticate all forms.
- Groups of companies can choose to have the same password. In order to comply with the Companies Act, the password must be delivered to Companies House in writing by the company, and signed by a serving officer of the company.

- When a form detailing the appointment of a director or company secretary is delivered, the appointee is required to indicate his or her consent to act as a director or secretary by providing three pieces of information which other people would not normally be expected to know. This information will not be displayed on the public file, but will be stored so that it can be retrieved should any question arise as to the validity of the appointment. Such personal information includes place of birth, mother's maiden name, NI number, passport number etc. Alternatively a director or company secretary may agree with Companies House a six-digit personal identification code.

More information

Handbook: Chapter 14. Manual: Chapter 10.
Companies House: http://www.companieshouse.gov.uk/ infoAndGuide/faq/webFiling.shtml .

Company secretary – appointment

Private companies need not appoint or retain a company secretary but may do so if they wish. Any provision in a private company's articles expressly requiring it to appoint a company secretary has been removed.

s.270
para.4 Sch.4
SI 2007/3495

Public companies must appoint a company secretary who must be qualified, see below.

ss 271, 273

The person named as company secretary, if any, on IN01 delivered on incorporation of a company is deemed to have been appointed as company secretary upon incorporation.

Subsequent appointments of company secretaries are made by the board of directors in accordance with the provisions of the Act or any provisions contained in their articles of association.

s.276

If a public company fails to appoint a company secretary, the Secretary of State may issue a direction requiring the appointment of a company and specifying the period in which the appointment must be made being between one and three months of the date of the direction.

s.272

Checklist

- The company's auditors cannot be appointed as company secretary.
- Company secretaries of public companies must be qualified by profession or experience.

s.1214

s.273

Procedure

- Convene a directors' meeting to approve the appointment of the company secretary. Ensure valid quorum present.
- File form AP03 or AP04 as appropriate.
- The necessary entry must be made in the Register of Secretaries.
- The company secretary is frequently a signatory on the company's bank account and accordingly it may be necessary to amend

s.276
s.275

the company's bank mandate in addition to notifying the bank of the new appointment and supplying specimen signatures to the bank.

■ The board will normally consider it necessary for the company secretary to have a service contract.

■ If the company secretary is to carry out executive duties, it may be considered necessary to include the company secretary on any policy of directors' and officers' indemnity insurance.

Filing requirement

■ Form AP03 or AP04 within 14 days

Notes

■ The appointment of a company secretary may be terminated by the directors. There is no need for shareholder approval. The company secretary may be able to bring an action for breach of contract in such circumstances and accordingly a compromise agreement may be appropriate.

■ The company secretary must provide a service address, which need not be their residential address. Unlike directors, there is no need to notify the company of their usual residential address.   s.277(1)

More information

⬛ Handbook: Chapter 3. ⬛ Manual: Chapter 11.

Company secretary – duties

Neither the Companies Acts nor the articles of association stipulate in any detail the duties of the company secretary. However, the company secretary is named as one of the persons who may sign prescribed forms and is an 'officer' of the company in terms of s.1262 of the Companies Act 2006.

Checklist

Although the company secretary has no specific statutory duties, the following are normally dealt with by the company secretary:

- Maintenance of statutory registers:
  - register of members;
  - register of charges;
  - minute books – shareholders and directors;
  - register of directors and secretaries;
  - register of debentures/stockholders, if appropriate.
- Completion of statutory forms (see page 237) as necessary, the most common forms being:
  - annual return;
  - changes in directors or secretaries;
  - change in registered office;
  - allotment of shares.
- Authenticating company documentation.
- Issue of share certificates or loan stock certificates.
- To ensure the safe keeping of the company seal and the company's copies of documentation, including:
  - directors' service contracts;
  - leases in respect of the company's property;
  - agreements, leases for office equipment, etc.;
  - documents of title, including share certificates, stock transfer forms, etc.
- As chief administrative officer the company secretary will often deal with:
  - employment of staff;
  - contracts relating to the company's premises and office equipment;

- □ the company's printing and stationery requirements;
- □ the company pension arrangements and employee share option schemes;
- □ company cars;
- □ management accounting.
- If the company secretary is not also a director of the company, he or she would not normally be involved in negotiating contracts and agreements relating to the company's trading activities.
- The company secretary should attend and take minutes of meetings of the board of directors and of shareholders. The company secretary, at the request of the chairman of the directors or of individual directors, will convene meetings of the directors and shareholders. The company secretary should advise the board of directors on technical compliance matters relating to the Companies Acts and other related issues.

Notes

- There are many other areas in which company secretaries can and often do become involved relating to the management of companies. However, as this book is directed towards the company law compliance aspects of a company secretary's role, these additional roles are not listed here. For a more comprehensive list readers should direct their enquiries to the Institute of Chartered Secretaries and Administrators, which has issued a guide entitled *The Duties of the Company Secretary*.

More information

Handbook: Chapter 3. Manual: Chapter 11.
Companies House: GBA1.

min

Crest settlement

Crest compliant articles is the term used to describe companies whose articles permit settlement in Crest, the dematerialised settlement system for shares of listed, AIM and Plus companies.

New applicants to these markets will be required to ensure that their articles are Crest compliant as a condition of entry. For existing companies, this could be by way of either a directors' or shareholders' resolution. For newly incorporated companies this power would be incorporated in the articles of association adopted for the purposes of admission.

Checklist

- Do the articles permit dematerialised holdings?

Procedure

- Convene a directors' meeting to approve appropriate resolution to amend the articles of association. Ensure valid quorum present.   reg.16 SI 2001/3755
- Alternatively, the amendments may be made by special resolution of the shareholders (see page 210).
- Where changes are made by directors' resolution, notice must be given to shareholders within 60 days of the date of the resolution.

Filing requirement

- Copy of directors' resolution or special resolution within 15 days.

Notes

- Enabling Crest settlement is the only occasion where the directors can resolve to change the company's articles of association.
- Prior to commencement of Crest settlement an application form must be submitted to Euroclear UK & Ireland Ltd, the system

operator, to enable Crest settlement. This process will usually be arranged by the company's share registrars.

More information

Handbook: Chapter 6. Manual: Chapter 5.

www.euroclear.com.

Debenture stock

The procedures for issuing, transferring, payment of interest on and redemption of debentures are broadly speaking the same as for the issuing of ordinary shares.

Debentures, unlike shares, are loans to the company, and are secured against the assets of the company.

Unless restricted by the articles of association, companies have an implied power to issue debentures.

Checklist

- Do articles restrict the directors' power to create and issue debentures?
- Create trust deed containing:
  - □ details of the stock, terms of issue, payment of interest, conversion into shares and/or redemption;
  - □ provisions constituting charges over the assets of the company in favour of the trust deed and giving details of the events by which the charge would be enforceable;
  - □ details of the trustees' powers to concur with the company in dealings with the charged assets;
  - □ where the security is by way of floating charge, a prohibition on the company issuing any further security ranking in priority to the debenture stock without previous consent;
  - □ details setting out the form of stock certificate, conditions of redemption, conversion rights and regulations in respect of the register of holders, transfer and transmission, and regulations for the conducting and holding of meetings of the debenture holders.
- Register allotment of debentures as soon as practical in register of debenture holders and in any event within two months of issue. s.741
- Ensure register available for inspection at the registered office or at a place specified by the company for inspections s.743
- If register not kept at registered office, file form AD02.

Procedure

- Convene a directors' meeting to approve the terms of the trust deed and the issue of debentures.
- The company secretary should arrange the preparation and issue of debenture stock certificates to each debenture holder.
- The company secretary should record the details of the debentures issued in the register of debenture holders.   s.741
- As debentures are secured on the assets of the company, the trust deed and form MG07 or MG08, as appropriate, must be submitted to Companies House within 21 days of the creation of the trust deed.   s.863

s.870(1)

Filing requirement

- Trust deed.
- Form MG07, MG08 within 21 days.
- Form AD02, if required.
- Filing fee £13.

More information

Handbook: Chapters 4 and 5. Manual: Chapter 9.

Directors – appointment

When a company is incorporated, the people named in the incorporation papers as directors and who have consented to act are deemed to be appointed on the date of incorporation. Following the appointment of these first directors, any further directors to be appointed should be appointed in accordance with the regulations laid down by the company's articles of association.

s.12

reg.17 Sch.1 or
reg.20 Sch.3
SI 2008/3229

In general, the articles will allow the existing directors to fill any casual vacancy in their number by themselves or by the members by ordinary resolution.

Occasionally, the articles of association will stipulate qualifications to be held for eligibility for appointment as a director. This used often to be a share qualification, although this is no longer a popular practice. Additional qualifications would more normally be the holding of a particular professional or technical qualification (e.g. chartered surveyor, architect, etc.).

All companies must have at least one director who is a natural person.

s.155

Checklist

- Check the articles of association to establish whether directors or only shareholders may appoint the new director(s).
- Check the articles to ensure any maximum number of directors stipulated in the articles has not already been reached.
- Is the proposed director at least 16 years old?

s.157

- If to be the sole director, is the proposed director a natural person?

s.155

- Is the director disqualified from acting by statute or the articles of association?
- Obtain the director's details required to complete form AP01 or AP02, including their residential address in addition to a service address.
- If appointment is as a non-executive to a listed company, ensure appropriate independence tests can be met if appropriate.

CC A3.1

- If directors' names are shown on the headed paper, this will need to be updated.
- Amend bank mandate if necessary.

Procedure

- Convene a directors' meeting to approve the appointment of a new director. Ensure valid quorum present.
- File completed form AP01 or AP02 at Companies House.
- Notify employees, customers, bank, if appropriate   s.167
- Notify Stock Exchange if company's shares are listed or traded on AIM.   LR16.7, AR
- Notify PLUS if company's shares are traded on the PLUS market.   PL
- Update the registers of directors and directors' residential addresses as necessary.   ss.163–165

Filing requirement

- Form AP01 or AP02 within 14 days.

Notes

- The new director should notify the board of any interest in contracts or other companies with which the company has dealings.   ss.177, 182
- The company secretary should inform the new director of the dates on which forthcoming board meetings are to be held, if these are known.
- If the articles of association require that the directors hold a share qualification, it is essential that the director acquires the appropriate shares within two months, or the time limit set down by the articles, if shorter.
- If the new director is to be an executive director, it may be considered necessary for the director to have a formal service contract with the company.
- It may be necessary to add the director to the company's directors' indemnity insurance policy, or indeed it may be necessary to effect such a policy.
- If this is the director's first appointment as director, he or she should be given guidance as to his or her duties and responsibilities in terms of the Companies Act and his or her duties and responsibilities to members.
- HM Revenue & Customs should be informed of the director's appointment.

More information

Handbook: Chapters 14 and 2. Manual: Chapter 11.

Directors – ceasing to hold office

A director may cease to hold office as a result of his or her death, by statute or under the provisions of the articles of association.

A director may be barred from holding or continuing to hold office as director for the following reasons:

- If the articles require that the director hold a share qualification and the director does not acquire the necessary shares within the time limit specified by the articles, if shorter.
- If the director becomes bankrupt (unless permitted to continue by the court).
- If the director is disqualified from holding a directorship by a court order.

Additionally, the articles may stipulate certain events which will require the director to vacate office, including:

- If a director resigns: resignation will not normally require consent of the remaining directors, although this may be required by the articles.
- If a director is absent from board meetings for a specific period without authority of the board.
- If a director has a receiving order made against him or if he enters into arrangements with his creditors.
- If the director is, or may be, suffering from a mental disorder and either the director has been admitted to hospital pursuant to the Mental Health Act or a court order has been made requiring his detention under the Act.
- If a director is removed from office by the remaining directors or by the members in some specified manner. This may include by written resolution of the remaining directors, by notice in writing of the company's holding company or in certain circumstances by their appointer. (For example, the holders of a particular class of shares may have the right to appoint a director and this person may be removed by them.)

In addition to the powers contained in the articles of association or   s.168

by statute, the shareholders of the company have the right at all times to remove a director by ordinary resolution. Care must be taken when using these provisions (see page 92).

Checklist

- The company's bankers should be informed and any necessary amendments made to the bank mandate.
- The company secretary should amend the company's register of directors and the register of directors' residential addresses.
- If the director's name is shown on the company's letter heading, this should be amended.
- If the company maintains a directors' indemnity insurance policy the insurers should be informed.
- The auditors should be informed.
- The HM Revenue & Customs should be notified.
- Any outstanding fees should be paid to the director and arrangements made for the return of any company property (car, computer equipment, etc.).
- If appropriate, the director should be reminded of any restrictions on his future employment contained in his contract of employment with the company.

ss162, 165

Procedure

- Convene a directors meeting to consider the circumstances of the director whose appointment has ceased. Ensure valid quorum present.
- File completed form TM01 at Companies House.
- Update register of directors and register of directors' residential addresses as necessary.
- Amend headed paper if directors' names are shown.
- Notify Stock Exchange if company's shares are listed or traded on AIM.
- Notify PLUS if company's shares are traded on the PLUS market.

ss.162, 165

LR16.7, AR

PL

Filing requirement

- Form TM01 within 14 days

More information

Handbook: Chapter 14. Manual: Chapter 11.

Enterprise Act 2002.
Company Directors' Disqualification Act 1986.
Insolvency Act 1986.

Directors – disqualification

The Company Directors Disqualification Act 1986 (CDDA 1986) consolidated a number of enactments relating to the disqualification of persons from being directors of companies and from being otherwise concerned with company management.

CDDA 1986 sets out circumstances where a court may or will (depending on the section) make a disqualification order that prohibits that person from being a director, liquidator or administrator of a company, a receiver or manager of a company's property or being in any way involved in the promotion, formation or management of a company for the specified period.

CDDA 1986
ss.1-6, 10

Under provisions introduced by the Insolvency Act 2000 a director facing prosecution may voluntarily apply to be disqualified as a director. This voluntary procedure speeds up the disqualification process and significantly reduces the costs for all parties.

Checklist

- Ensure the court order or copy bears the seal of the court.
- The company's bankers should be informed, and any necessary amendments made to the bank mandate.
- The secretary should amend the company's register of directors.
- If the director's name is shown on the company's letter heading, this should be amended.
- If the company maintains a directors' indemnity insurance policy, the insurers should be informed.
- The auditors, if any, should be informed.
- HM Revenue & Customs should be notified.
- Any outstanding fees should be paid to the director and arrangements made for the return of any company property (car, computer equipment, etc.).
- If appropriate, the director should be reminded of any restrictions on his future employment contained in his contract of employment with the company.

Form DQ01

Procedure

- File completed form TM01 at Companies House   s.167
- Update register of directors as necessary.
- Amend headed paper if directors names are shown.
- Notify Stock Exchange if company's shares are listed or traded   LR16.7
  on AIM.
- Notify Plus Markets Group if company's shares are traded on the
  Plus market.

Filing requirement

- Form TM01 within 14 days.   s.167
- Copy of disqualification order.

More information

⬚Handbook: Chapter 2. ▤ Manual: Chapter 11.

Directors – duties

A director's prime duty, which he holds together with his fellow directors, is to manage the company for the benefit of its members. The directors may delegate some or all of their powers to particular directors (perhaps constituting a committee of the board) and/or other senior officers in the company, but they cannot delegate their duties.

The Companies Act 2006 introduced four duties of directors on 1 October 2007, and a further three came into effect on 1 October 2008. These duties codify, with some amendments, existing case law.

The directors must ensure that suitable arrangements are in place to enable the company to meet its statutory duties and are liable to penalties if the company is in default. Directors of many companies will delegate these duties to the company secretary and as it is the directors who are liable in the event of default, care must be taken to ensure that the company secretary is suitably qualified.

In many small private companies the directors will often rely on their professional advisers to undertake some of their responsibilities, such as filing accounts and preparation of annual return. Directors must act on the advice of their advisers so as to ensure that the statutory obligations are met. It is the directors and not the professional advisers who are liable, and in the event of default and prosecution it is the directors who will be called to account.

Checklist

The seven statutory duties are:

To act within their powers

s.171

- Directors must act in accordance with the company's constitution and only exercise powers for the purposes for which they are conferred. The company's articles of association should be consulted to ascertain the extent of a director's powers and any limitations placed upon them.

To promote the success of the company

s.172

■ A director must act in the way he considers, in good faith, would be most likely to promote the success of the company for the benefit of its members as a whole, and in doing so have regard (amongst other matters) to:
  □ the likely consequences of any decision in the long term;
  □ the interests of the company's employees;
  □ the need to foster the company's business relationships with suppliers, customers and others;
  □ the impact of the company's operations on the community and the environment;
  □ the desirability of the company maintaining a reputation for high standards of business conduct; and the need to act fairly as between members of the company.

To exercise independent judgement

s.173

■ A director must exercise independent judgement.
■ This duty is not infringed by him acting in accordance with an agreement duly entered into by the company that restricts the future exercise of discretion by its directors; or in a way authorised by the company's constitution.

To exercise reasonable care, skill and diligence

s.174

■ The duties imposed by ss.173 and 174 require that a director owes a duty to exercise the same standard of care, skill and diligence that would be exercised by a reasonably diligent person with:

  the general knowledge, skill and experience that may reasonably be expected of the person carrying out the same functions as a director in relation to that company (an objective test); and

■ the general knowledge, skill and experience that the director actually has (a subjective test).
■ For example, a finance director would be expected to have a greater knowledge of finance issues than, say, the HR director (the objective test); but if the HR director is also a qualified accountant, then he would be expected to have a greater knowledge than would normally be expected of a HR director although not necessarily the same knowledge as the finance director (the subjective test).

To avoid conflicts of interest

s.175

■ Directors must avoid situations in which they have or might have a direct or indirect interest that conflicts or might conflict with the interests of the company. Of particular importance are conflicts relating to property, information or opportunity, regardless of whether the company could take advantage of such opportunities.

s.175(2)

■ The duty does not apply to conflicts arising out of transactions or arrangement between the company and the director.

■ Where the company is a private company, authorisation may be given by resolution of the directors provided there is nothing in the company's articles of association which invalidated the authorisation.

■ Where the company is a public company, authorisation may be given by resolution of the directors, provided there is specific authority in the company's articles of association which permit directors to authorise such transactions.

■ Such authorisation, whether for a private or public company, is only valid if the necessary quorum for a meeting of the directors is present excluding the director with the conflict of interest and without that director voting.

s.175(6)

Not to accept benefits from third parties

s.176

■ Directors must not accept a benefit from a third party being given by virtue of their being a director or due to any action or inaction by the director.

■ Benefits received by a director from a person by whom his services are provided are not to be regarded as paid by a third party.

■ The duty is not infringed if the acceptance of the benefit cannot reasonably be regarded as likely to give rise to a conflict of interest.

To declare interests in any proposed transaction or arrangement

s.177

■ A director must declare the full nature and extent of any direct or indirect interest in any proposed transaction or arrangement before that transaction or arrangement is entered into. The declaration may be given at a meeting of the directors or by general notification on appointment.

ss.184,185

■ Where a previous notification or interest becomes inaccurate or incomplete, additional notification(s) must be made.

- Notification is not required where the director is not aware of the interest or is not aware of the transaction or arrangement.
- Notification is not required where the nature of the interest is such that it cannot reasonably be regarded as likely to give rise to a conflict of interest, to the extent that the other directors are already aware of the interest without requiring specific notification or where the transaction relates to the director's service contract.

More information

Handbook: Chapter 2. Manual: Chapter 11.
Companies House GBA1

Directors' meetings – private companies

There are no fixed rules regarding operation of the board of directors. The articles of association will govern the powers of directors. The maximum or minimum number of directors and the quorum necessary for meetings of the directors will be stipulated.

regs 7–16 Sch.1
SI 2008/3229

Meetings of the directors should be held upon 'reasonable' notice, according to the circumstances of the company or the meeting concerned. Where the board of directors all work in the same office, reasonable notice may well be two or three hours. Where the directors normally meet on a quarterly basis only, and do not work at the same location, then reasonable notice may be two weeks, or longer.

Meetings are usually called by the company secretary on instructions of the chairman, although any director may request that a meeting be convened, or convene it themselves.

reg.9 Sch.1
SI 2008/3229

Votes at a directors' meeting are taken on the basis of one vote per director. All resolutions are passed by a simple majority. The articles of association of the company may give the chairman a casting vote in circumstances where there is an equal number of votes both for and against a particular resolution.

regs 7,8,13
SI 2008/3229

In certain circumstances, usually where one or other directors have provided the majority of the company's funding, the articles may provide for enhanced voting rights for certain specified directors.

regs 65–69
Table A
SI 1985/805

Directors may be empowered by the articles of association to appoint someone to attend and vote in their place, when circumstances dictate that they are unable to attend the meeting themselves. Such authority is not contained in the CA 2006 model articles, although was contained in Table A for companies incorporated prior to 1 October 2009.

In addition to reaching decisions at meetings, the model articles permit private company directors to reach decisions by indicating to each other by any means that they share a common view on any particular matter. Although many formal matters may be decided

reg.8(2) Sch.1
SI 2008/3229

upon by circulating written resolutions where a contentious matter requires consideration and an exchange of views, it is important to ensure that all directors are able to participate fully in that debate

Although the day-to-day running of the company will be left to the managing director and the other executive directors, the board should meet to decide upon matters of policy and matters requiring signature on behalf of the board.

Checklist

- Pre-CA 2006 articles may provide for directors not in the UK not to be entitled to receive notice of meetings.
- Has notice been given to all directors entitled to notice?
- Have all relevant board papers been circulated sufficiently in advance of the meeting?
- At the meeting, is a quorum present at the start and throughout the meeting?
- Have participating directors declared any conflicts of interest and considered their statutory duties in reaching their decision?
- Have minutes been taken and once approved recorded in the minute book?

reg.11 Sch.1
SI 2008/3229
reg.16 Sch.3
SI 2008/3229
ss.171 –177
reg.15 Sch.1 SI
2006/3229
s.248

Notes

- Shareholders have no right to view the minutes of the directors.

More information

Handbook: Chapter 2. Manual: Chapter 13.
Companies House: GBA7 – Resolutions only.

Directors' meetings – public companies

There are no fixed rules regarding operation of the board of directors. The articles of association will govern the powers of directors. The maximum or minimum number of directors and the quorum necessary for meetings of the directors will be stipulated.

regs 7–19 Sch.3
SI 2008/3229

Meetings of the directors should be held upon 'reasonable' notice, according to the circumstances of the company or the meeting concerned. Where the board of directors all work in the same office, reasonable notice may well be two or three hours. Where the directors normally meet on a quarterly basis only and do not work at the same location, then reasonable notice may be two weeks, or more.

Meetings are usually called by the company secretary on instructions of the chairman, although any director may request that a meeting be convened or convene it themselves.

reg.8 Sch.3
SI 2008/3229

Votes at a directors' meeting are taken on the basis of one vote per director. All resolutions are passed by a simple majority. The articles of association of the company may give the chairman a casting vote in circumstances where there is an equal number of votes both for and against a particular resolution.

regs 13,14
SI 2008/3229

In certain circumstances, usually where one or other directors have provided the majority of the company's funding, the articles may provide for enhanced voting rights for certain specified directors.

Directors may be empowered by the articles of association to appoint someone to attend and vote in their place, when circumstances dictate that they are unable to attend the meeting themselves. If a director is appointed as an alternate for another director, that director will have two votes and may cast each vote differently.

reg.15 Sch.3
SI 2008/3229

In addition to reaching decisions at meetings, the model articles permit public company directors to reach decisions by any other means, provided they can communicate with each other. Accordingly decisions may be reached by conference video or telephone facilities. Written resolutions of directors are permitted by the

reg.9(1)(b) Sch.3
SI 2008/3229

regs 17,18 Sch.3
SI 2008/3229 model articles. As decisions may require an exchange of views, it is important to ensure that all directors are able to participate fully in that debate

Although the day-to-day running of the company will be left to the managing director and the other executive directors, the board should meet to decide upon matters of policy and matters requiring signature on behalf of the board.

Checklist

- Pre-CA 2006 articles may provide for directors not in the UK not to be entitled to receive notice of meetings.
- Has notice been given to all directors entitled to notice?
- Have participating directors declared any conflicts of interest and considered their statutory duties in reaching their decision?   reg.16 Sch.3 SI 2008/3229 ss.171–177
- Have all relevant board papers been circulated sufficiently in advance of the meeting?   ss.
- At the meeting, is a quorum present at the start and throughout the meeting?   reg.10 Sch.3 SI 2008/3229
- Have minutes been taken and once approved, recorded in the minute book?   s.248

Notes

- Shareholders have no right to view the minutes of the directors.

More information

Handbook: Chapter 2. Manual: Chapter 13.
Companies House: GBA7 – Resolutions only.

Directors – removal

Irrespective of any provisions contained in the company's articles of association or a director's service contract, the shareholders can, at any time, remove a director by ordinary resolution.

s.168

Checklist

- Will the director resign?
- Check the articles to see if the director can be removed by a vote of the remaining directors or by notice from say the holding company.
- Is the director due to retire by rotation at the next annual general meeting. (public companies only)?
- Special notice (see page 210) of the proposed removal needs to be given to the company by an officer.

s.168(2)

- The director whose removal is proposed must be sent a copy of the special notice.

s.169(1)

Procedure

- Company secretary, director or a shareholder to give special notice to the company of proposal to remove a director. The special notice must be received at least 28 clear days before the meeting.

s.169(1)

- If the removal is proposed by shareholders, it may be appropriate for them to requisition a general meeting as well (see page 110).

s.303

- A copy of the special notice must be sent to the director whose removal has been proposed.

s.169(1)

- Then convene a board meeting to consider the special notice and convene a general meeting if appropriate.
- The company secretary or a director to issue a notice convening a general meeting on 14 clear days' notice to consider the resolution as an ordinary resolution. The notice should state on it that special notice has been given. The director whose removal is proposed is entitled to have a written representation circulated with the notice.

s.168

s.169(3)

- If the resolution is approved, file form TM01 with Companies House.

- The company secretary should ensure that the register of directors is amended.
- Listed, AIM or Plus companies must make an appropriate announcement no later than the day following the removal.

Filing requirement

- Form TM01 within 14 days.

Notes

- The director to be removed has the right to be heard at the general meeting even if he or she is not a shareholder.
- Although the meeting can be held at short notice without contravening the provisions relating to the giving of special notice, this may be seen as prejudicial to the director's case, and care must be taken when convening the meeting on short notice.
- Although the shareholders can remove the director from office, this would not prejudice the director's rights under any service contract, nor would it affect his or her right to take action against the company for any breach.
- The removal of a director must be put to a meeting of the members and cannot be dealt with by means of a written resolution by a private company.

s.168(1)

More information

Handbook: Chapter 2. Manual: Chapter 11.

Directors – residential address

Directors (and in the case of an overseas company registered in Great Britain, a representative) must give details of a service address on form AP01 and any change in that address on form CH01. s.167

If the service address of a director is not their usual residential address, the director must notify the company of their usual residential address, and the company must maintain a register of directors' residential addresses. Where the service address is their usual residential address, the register of directors' residential addresses need only contain an entry to that effect. s.165

Although details of the residential address are contained in form AP01, those details are not disclosed on the public file unless required by a court order, or where the Registrar has cause to believe that the service address is not effective at bringing documents to the notice of the director. ss.240–246

More information

Handbook: Chapter 2. Manual: Chapter 11.
Companies House: GBA1.

Dissolution

The Registrar is authorised by the Act to remove from the register those companies that he or she believes are defunct. This procedure will frequently be used where a company has failed to file accounts or annual returns, and no response is received to letters sent to the company's registered office. s.1000

In addition the directors of a company may voluntarily request that the company be struck off. s.1003

This procedure may not be used if, within three months of the proposed application, the company has changed its name, traded, disposed of property or rights for value, or engaged in any activity other than that required to effect the dissolution, or where application for a scheme of arrangement or petition or order under the Insolvency Act has been made. s.1004 s.1005

Checklist

- Does the company have any assets or liabilities, or hold title to any property or assets?
- During the three months preceding the application, has the company:
  - ☐ changed its name?
  - ☐ traded?
  - ☐ disposed of any property or rights for value?
  - ☐ engaged in any activity other than that required to effect the dissolution?
- Check that insolvency or administration procedures have not commenced.

Procedure

- Convene a directors' meeting to consider the dissolution of the company.
- If part of a group, enter into a transfer of assets agreement with another group company to 'sweep up' any assets not previously disposed of.

File completed form DS01 at Companies House signed by all directors, where there are two or less, or a majority of directors, if there are three or more.

A copy of the application must be sent within seven days to any person who at any time on or after the date of application but prior to dissolution or withdrawal was: ss.1006, 1007
   - □ an employee; or
   - □ a member; or
   - □ a creditor; or
   - □ a director; or
   - □ a manager or trustee of any pension fund established for the employees.
- VAT registered companies must notify their VAT office.
- On receipt of the application the Registrar will publish a notice in the *Gazette* inviting any objections as to why the company should not be struck off.
- If no objections are made within three months of publication in the *Gazette*, the Registrar will strike off the company and publish a further notice in the *Gazette* notifying that the company has been dissolved.   s.1003(3)

Filing requirement

- Form DS01.
- £10 filing fee.

Notes

- The directors may halt the dissolution process by submitting form DS02.   ss.1009, 1010
- Care must be taken to ensure that there are no assets remaining in the company, as these will pass to the Crown on dissolution. Within groups of companies, leases are frequently left in the name of dormant subsidiaries.
- Where the company has only recently ceased to trade, it will be necessary to contact the company's corporation tax office to settle any liability to tax or confirm that no tax is due, otherwise HM Revenue & Customs are likely to object to the dissolution as a matter of course.

More information

Handbook: Chapter 1. Manual: Chapter 19.

Dividends

Unless shares of any particular class carry a fixed dividend, the declaration and payment of a dividend is at the directors' discretion as set out in the company's articles.

reg.30(2) Sch.1 SI 2008/3229 (ltd co)

Dividends can be paid only if the company has sufficient distributable profits.

reg.70(2) Sch.3 SI 2008/3229 (Plc); s.830

The directors may declare a dividend as they see fit, in the case of an interim dividend, or subject to the approval of the members by ordinary resolution, in the case of the final dividend.

reg.30 Sch.1, reg.70 Sch.3 SI 2008/3229

The declaration of any dividend should be made by reference to the relevant accounts. These would normally be the most recent annual accounts, except where those accounts show that there is insufficient profit available or the dividend is proposed to be paid in the first accounting period. In such cases, interim or initial accounts, as appropriate, will be required. If the annual accounts have a qualified auditors' report the auditors must issue a statement as to whether the qualification is material in determining if a distribution can be made, in terms of s.836.

s.836(2)

s.837(4)

For a private company, the interim or initial accounts must enable a reasonable judgement to be made as to the availability of distributable reserves.

ss.838(1), 839(1)

For a public company those accounts must be properly prepared in accordance with ss.395 to 397 of the Act. Where interim accounts are prepared, these must be signed and a copy filed with the Registrar of Companies. In the case of initial accounts these must contain a report from the company's auditors and if the audit report is qualified, a statement from the auditors as to whether the qualification is material in determining if a distribution can be made, in terms of s.836. A copy of the signed accounts, audit report and any statement, if required, must be laid before the members in general meeting and delivered to the Registrar of Companies.

s.838(2)–(6)

s.839(2)–(7)

Checklist

- Dividends are usually declared, stating both a record date and a later payment date. The record date establishes a date on which the entitlements are to be calculated, and any changes in ownership after that date are ignored.

- On the payment date, dividend cheques and tax vouchers should be completed and issued to members.
- Dividend payments have an associated tax credit in respect of part of the corporation tax paid or to be paid on the profit. Subject to their own circumstances, individual members can apply this tax credit to reduce the tax payable by them on the distribution. The tax credit is equal to one-ninth of the amount payable to each member.

Procedure

Interim dividend

- Convene a directors' meeting to consider the payment of an interim dividend. Ensure sufficient distributable profit is available by reference to relevant accounts.
- The company secretary arranges the printing of dividend warrants and tax vouchers.
- Dividend warrants and tax vouchers are despatched to the shareholders.

Final dividend

- Accounts and notice of general meeting are issued to members. If accounts have a qualified audit report, the auditors' statement on their qualification is circulated with the accounts.
- The general meeting is held.
- If approval is given to the final dividend, the company secretary arranges payment in the same way as for an interim dividend. Although members can reduce the amount of dividend payable, they cannot approve a payment at a higher rate than recommended by the directors.

Filing requirement

- Interim or initial accounts, if prepared by a public company.

ss.838(6), 839(7)

Notes

- The secretary should liaise with their bank, or if relevant their share registrars, concerning the format of the dividend warrant.

- Schedule of payments and non-cashed cheques must be maintained.
- Often companies maintain a separate dividend account as once declared and dividend cheques issued, the uncashed funds are no longer a company asset.

More information

Handbook: Chapter 7. Manual: Chapter 7.

Documents – suggested retention periods

Type of document	Period of retention	
Statutory records		
Certificate of incorporation	Original to be kept permanently	
Certificate to commence business (public company)	Original to be kept permanently	
Articles of association	Original to be kept permanently	
Seal book/register	Original to be kept permanently	
Register of directors and secretaries	Original to be kept permanently	s.162
Register of directors' residential addresses	Original to be kept permanently	s.165
Register of interests in voting shares,		s.808
Register of charges,		s.876
Register of members	Current members permanently	s.113
	Former members ten years	s.121
Register of debenture or loan stock holders	Original to be kept permanently	s.743
Meeting records		
Minutes of general and class meetings, written resolutions	Originals to be kept permanently for meetings that were held prior to 1/10/2007	Para.40 Sch.1 SI 2007/2194
	Ten years after meeting for meetings held after 1/10/2007	s.248(2)
Directors' minutes	Originals to be kept permanently for meetings that were held prior to 1/10/2007	
	Ten years after meeting for meetings held after 1/10/2007	
Circulars to shareholders including notices of meetings	Master copy to be kept permanently	
Proxy forms/polling cards	One month if no poll demanded; one year if poll demanded	

Type of document	Period of retention	
Accounting and financial records		
Annual report and accounts	Signed copy to be kept permanently (a stock of spare copies should be maintained for up to five years to meet casual requests)	
Accounting records required by the Companies Acts	Six years for a public company; three years for a private company	s.388(4)(b) s.388(4)(a)
Taxation returns and records	Six years	
Internal financial reports	Six years	
Statements and instructions to banks	Six years	
Tax returns	Permanently	
Expense accounts	Seven years	
Customs and Excise returns	Six years	
Share registration documents	Refer to articles but typical periods are: Forms for application of shares, debentures, etc., forms of acceptance and transfer, renounceable letters of acceptance and allotment, renounceable share certificates request for designation or redesignation of accounts, letters of request, allotment sheets letters of indemnity for lost share certificates, stop notices and other court orders six years from date of registration	reg.82 Sch.3 SI 2008/3229
Powers of attorney	Ten years after cessation of membership to which power relates	s.121
Dividend and interest bank mandate forms	Two years after registration	
Cancelled share or stock certificates	One year after cancellation	
Notification of change of address	Two years	
Any contract or memorandum to purchase the company's own shares	Ten years	
Report of an interest in voting shares for investigations requisitioned by members	Six years	

Type of document	Period of retention
Register of interest in shares when company ceases to be a public company	Six years

Property records

Deeds of title	Permanently
Leases	Twelve years after lease has terminated
Agreements with architects, builders, etc.	Six years after contract completion
Patent and trade mark records	Permanently

HR records

Staff personnel records	Seven years after employment ceases
Patent agreements with staff	Twenty years after employment ceases
Applications for jobs	Up to 12 months
Payroll records	Twelve years
Salary registers	Six years
Employment agreements	Permanently
Time cards and piecework records	Two years
Wages records	Six years
Medical records	Twelve years
Industrial training records	Six years
Accident books	Twelve years

Pension records

Trustees and rules (pension schemes)	Permanently
Trustees' minute book	Permanently
Pension fund annual accounts and Inland Revenue approvals	Permanently
Investment records	Permanently
Actuarial valuation records	Permanently
Contribution records	Permanently
Records of ex-pensioners	Six years after cessation of benefit
Pension scheme investment policies	Twelve years after cessation

Insurance records

Group health policies	Twelve years after final cessation of benefit
Group personal accident policies	Twelve years after cessation of benefit

Type of document	*Period of retention*
Public liability policies	Permanently
Product liability policies	Permanently
Employers' liability policies	Permanently
Sundry insurance policies	Three years after lapse
Claims correspondence	Three years after settlement
Accident reports and relevant correspondence	Three years after settlement
Insurance schedules	Ten years

Other records

Vehicle registration records, MOT certificates and vehicle	Two years after disposal of vehicle maintenance records
Certificates and other documents of title	Permanently, or until investment disposed of
Trust deeds	Originals to be kept permanently
Contracts with customers, suppliers or agents	Six years after expiry
Licensing agreements	Six years after expiry
Rental and hire purchase agreements	Six years after expiry
Indemnities and guarantees	Six years after expiry

Dormant companies

Where a company has not traded during any particular financial period, the company can dispense with the obligation to prepare audited accounts and need only file an abbreviated balance sheet and notes with Companies House. This is a separate dispensation from the audit exemptions considered on page 11.

s.480

Checklist

- There must have been no transactions required to be made in the company's accounting records.
- The company must not be:
  - ☐ an authorised insurance company, a banking company or e-money issuer, MiFID investment firm or a UCITS management company; or
  - ☐ carrying on insurance market activity;
  - ☐ required to prepare group accounts.
- The company must qualify as a small company (see page 18), or would have but for the fact that it is:
  - ☐ a public company;
  - ☐ a member of an ineligible group.
- Balance sheet must contain statements immediately above the directors signature(s) that:
  - ☐ the company is entitled to the exemption;
  - ☐ the directors acknowledge their responsibilities;
  - ☐ the accounts give a true and fair view;
  - ☐ the members have not required the accounts to be audited (this only applies to the set of accounts filed at companies house).

s.1169

s.481

s.480(2)(b)
s.480(2)(a)

s.475(2)
s.475(3)(b)
s.396(2)
s.475(3)(a)

Procedure

- Non-trading non-audited accounts must be prepared.
- Convene a directors' meeting to approve the accounts.
- Signed copy to be filed with the Registrar within the same timescales for a trading company (see page 5).

Filing requirement

- Copy of the accounts within the appropriate timescale: six months for a public company and nine months for a private company.

Notes

- To remain dormant, any costs must be paid by someone other than the company itself and any cash held in a bank must be in a non-interest-bearing account.
- Receipt of payment by the company for the shares taken by the subscribers or any payment made in respect of any change of name, re-registration fees, annual returns or late filing penalties may be disregarded for the purposes of assessing whether a company is dormant. s.1169(3)
- Although the copy that is filed with the Registrar may be abbreviated and not contain a directors' report, the copy circulated to shareholders must be full accounts and accordingly a directors' report will be required.

More information

Handbook: Chapter 10. Manual: Chapter 15.

Electronic communications

Subject to any provisions in their articles, companies may send written resolutions, notices, annual accounts and related documents to their members in hard copy, in electronic form or by making the documents available for download from a website.

ss.293(2), 308, 309

When making written resolutions available on a website these are not valid unless the document(s) are available throughout the period commencing with the circulation date and ending on the date the resolution lapses.

s.299

Notice of a meeting given by publication on a website is not valid unless the notification sent to members states that it concerns a notice of a general meeting, specifies the place, date and time of the meeting, and in the case of a public company AGM, states that the meeting is to be an AGM. The documents must be available throughout the period commencing on the date of notification and ending at the conclusion of the meeting.

s.309

Notification of the website address may be given in hard copy or by electronic communication provided the member has provided an address for that purpose.

Quoted companies are required to make their annual report and accounts available on a website as soon as reasonably practical and ending no earlier than the date the following annual report and accounts are made available on the website.

s.430

Any member receiving documents or information by electronic communication or by publication on a website they can request that they receive copies of documents in hard copy and the company must supply those copies within 21 days.

s.1145

More information

 Manual: Chapter 14.

Forfeiture

When shares have been allotted as either nil or partly paid, the balance outstanding on the shares can be called at any time by the directors (see page 50). The amount of this call can be all or part of the balance outstanding.

Any shares on which a call has been made and which remains outstanding may be forfeited, provided there is authority in the company articles. Companies that have adopted Table A under previous Companies Acts and public companies incorporated after 1 October 2009 and adopting the model articles for a public company will have such provisions in their articles. A private company incorporated after 1 October 2009 and adopting the model articles for a private company will not have such provisions in their articles, as reg.21 of the model articles for private company only permits shares to be issued fully paid.

reg.12–22
Table A
CA 1985
reg.54–62
Sch.3
SI 2008/3229

The procedures for making a call and subsequent forfeiture must be strictly adhered to. If they are not, the court may overturn any forfeiture. The provisions under which shares may be forfeited are contained in the company's articles of association.

Checklist

- Check the articles of association.

Procedure (taken from the model articles for public companies)

- If a call notice has not been paid and forfeiture is to be implemented, the directors must first give the members notice.
- The company secretary to issue a notice to the member(s), giving not less than 14 days' notice requiring payment of all outstanding amounts, and must state that if the notice is not complied with, the shares are liable to forfeiture.
- If the call remains unpaid, convene a board meeting to consider forfeiture of the shares. This is accomplished by the directors resolving that the shares be forfeited.

- Notice of forfeiture is usually sent to the member(s) by the company secretary, but it is not a requirement.
- Forfeited shares may be sold or cancelled, as the directors see fit.
- Details of the forfeiture must be entered in the register of members.

Filing requirement

- None.

Notes

- If the shareholder cannot or will not pay the call, he or she may wish to surrender the shares. Shares can only be surrendered if they are already liable to be forfeited.
- The member whose shares have been forfeited ceases to be a member in respect of such shares as soon as the forfeiture has been entered in the register of members. Such a person does, however, remain liable for any amounts unpaid on the shares.
- Forfeited shares may be sold or disposed of on such terms and in such manner as the directors think fit. Forfeited shares that are reissued must be issued at a price not less than the amounts remaining unpaid. When shares are reissued, the original member will no longer be liable for the uncalled amounts once the full amount has been received by the company, from whatever source.   s.662
- Where the shares are reissued at a price greater than the unpaid amount, then the company shall pay to the original member the additional monies received, up to the amount paid by them.
- At the end of the financial year it will be necessary to inform the auditors that certain shares have been forfeited and whether or not they have been reissued.

More information

Handbook: Chapter 5. Manual: Chapter 2.

General meetings

All meetings of members of a private company are a general meeting unless there are express provisions in its articles that provide for it to hold an annual general meeting or an extraordinary general meeting.

s.301

Any meeting of a public company which is not an annual general meeting is a general meeting. If there is express provision in its articles, an extraordinary general meeting may be held. Where an extraordinary general meeting is held there is no longer any distinction between that and a general meeting.

s.336

All matters that can be considered at a general meeting of a private company may be undertaken by written resolution with the exception of considering resolutions for the removal of a director or of auditors.

Procedure

- Convene a board meeting to consider the business to be put to shareholders, and convene a general meeting if appropriate.

s.302

- The company secretary or a director to issue a notice convening the general meeting on 14 clear days' notice. If appropriate, the notice should state on it that special notice has been given.

s.307

- The meeting may be held upon shorter notice if 90 per cent of the members entitled to attend and vote agree, in the case of a private company, and 95 per cent for a public company general meeting.

s.307(5)

Filing requirement

- Copies of resolutions and appropriate forms within 15 days.

s.30

More information

Handbook: Chapter 9. Manual: Chapter 14.

General meetings – requisition

Subject to the company's articles of association, a member or members holding not less than 10 per cent of the paid-up issued share capital and carrying the right to vote may requisition a meeting of the members. In the case of a private company, if more than 12 months have passed since the previous general meeting, the required percentage is reduced to 5 per cent. s.303(3)

s.303(3)

If the directors do not convene a meeting within 21 days of receiving the requisition, those who have requisitioned it may convene the meeting themselves for a date not more than three months thereafter. s.305

The directors are deemed not to have duly convened the meeting if it is convened for a date more than 28 days after the date of the notice convening the meeting. s.304

Checklist

- Do the requisitionists hold the necessary number of shares?
- Has notice of the requisition been served on the company, either in hard copy or electronic form, and has it been authenticated by the requisitionist(s)? s.303(6)
- The request must state the general nature of the business to be considered, and may included the text of a resolution that may be properly moved at the meeting. s.303(4)
- A resolution may be properly moved unless it would be ineffective due to inconsistency with any legislation or the company's constitution, or it is defamatory, frivolous or vexatious. s.303(5)

Procedure

- A letter or electronic communication of requisition and the text of the desired resolution(s) or general nature of the business must be delivered to the company.
- Convene a board meeting to consider the request and convene a general meeting if appropriate. If a meeting has been requested, it is not sufficient for the directors of a private company to circulate the proposed resolution as a written resolution.

- The directors must convene the meeting within 21 days of receipt. If approved, the company secretary or a director is to issue a notice convening a general meeting to be held within 28 days, on appropriate notice, to consider the resolution(s).

s.304

Filing requirements

- There are no requirments specific to the meeting having been requested, but it will be necessary to file copies of any special resolutions or ordinary resolutions meeting the criteria set out in s.29 within 15 days.

More information

Handbook: Chapter 9. Manual: Chapter 14.

Headed paper

The full name of the company as registered must be shown on all letters, notices and other official publications, emails, its website, bills of exchange, promissory notes, cheques and orders for money or goods signed by or on behalf of the company, invoices, receipts and letters of credit. If this provision is not complied with, the signatory of the document in question may be personally liable in the event of default by the company.

s.82

regs 6, 7
SI 2008/495

Where the company operates under a trading name other than its registered name, the registered name will usually be shown at the foot of the page.

Checklist

- Company name as registered.
- The place of registration must be shown, e.g. registered in England and Wales, Cardiff, Wales, Scotland or Edinburgh.
- The company's registration number.
- The address of the company's registered office. Where the company's business address and registered office are the same, the fact that the address shown on the headed paper is the registered office must be stated unless the address of the registered office is shown separately.
- Where the company is an investment company, this fact must be stated on the headed paper.
- In the case of a charity where the company's name does not include the word 'Charity' or 'Charitable', the fact that it is a charity must be stated on the headed paper. If this provision is not complied with, the signatory to any documents may be personally liable in the event of any default by the company.
- Where directors' names are shown on headed paper, all the directors' names must be shown, and not just some of them. This is particularly important to remember where the directors have personalised stationery. It is not necessary to show the nationality of directors.
- If the company has been permitted not to include the word

'limited' in its registered name, then the headed paper must disclose that the company is a limited company.
- If the company is an investment company, this must be disclosed.

Filing requirement

- None.

Notes

- When a company changes its registered office, the company's headed paper must be changed to show the new address within 14 days of the date of change. The date of change is the date of registration of form AD01 by the Registrar of Companies.   s.87(3)
- Although not necessary, if there is a reference to the company's share capital on the headed paper, this must be to the paid-up share capital.   reg.7(3) SI 2008/495

More information

Handbook: Chapter 1. Manual: Chapter 1.

HM Revenue & Customs – Stamp Duty Office

Except in cases where the transaction is exempt from stamp duty, all stock transfer forms with a transfer value of £1,000 or more must be stamped by HM Revenue & Customs.

Companies must not register transfers that are liable to duty if not stamped, as registering such a transfer does not give good title to the underlying shares.

For all enquiries, please contact HM Revenue & Customs' dedicated enquiry line number: 0121 616 4513.

Written enquires should be addressed to the Customer Service office:

Customer Service Manager
HMRC Birmingham Stamp Office
9th Floor
City Centre House
30 Union Street
Birmingham
B2 4AR

More information

Handbook: Chapter 6. Manual: Chapter 5.

HM Revenue & Customs: www.hmrc.gov.uk/so.

ICSA Code on Good Boardroom Practice

Reliance on unwritten boardroom procedures and practices is no longer acceptable in the modern business environment. Whilst it is acknowledged that company law should not attempt to prescribe any particular style of boardroom management, certain basic principles of good boardroom practice can be considered to be universally applicable.

The Institute of Chartered Secretaries and Administrators (ICSA) has formulated a Code for directors and company secretaries as a guide to the matters that it believes should be addressed and, wherever applicable, accepted formally by boards of directors in recognition of a commitment to adhere to an overall concept of best practice. Although particularly relevant to public companies with external shareholders, all companies will benefit by observing the Code's provisions.

Boardroom procedures should be periodically reviewed to ensure both the satisfactory operation of the Code and the identification of matters which individual companies could advantageously bring within its scope.

Checklist

- Establish written procedures:
    - ☐ Provide each director with a copy.
    - ☐ Monitor compliance and report breaches to the board.
- All new directors to be given appropriate induction to enable them to perform their duties.
- Guidance for non-executive directors should include procedures:
    - ☐ for obtaining information.
    - ☐ for requisitioning a board meeting.
- In the conduct of board business:
    - ☐ all directors should receive the same information at the same time.
    - ☐ all directors should be given sufficient time to consider the information.

- Identify matters reserved to the board and lay down procedures when a decision is required before its next meeting.
- All material contracts, and especially those not in the ordinary course of business, should be referred to the board.
- The board should approve definitions of 'material' and 'not in the ordinary course of business'.
- Agenda for individual meetings of the board to be settled by the chairman in consultation with the company secretary.
- The company secretary should be responsible to the chairman for the proper administration of meetings of the company, the board and any committees thereof.
- The minutes of meetings should record the decisions taken and provide sufficient background to those decisions.
- All papers presented at meetings should be identified and retained for reference.
- Minutes of committees meetings should be circulated to the board.
- Where the articles of association allow the board to delegate any of its powers to a committee, the board should approve:
  - □ the membership and quorum of any such committee.
  - □ its terms of reference.
  - □ the extent of any powers delegated to it.
- Any director or the company secretary must be able raise at any board meeting any matter whether or not on the agenda for the meeting.

More information

Handbook: Appendix 3. Manual: Chapter 12.

ICSA Code on Good Boardroom Practice.

ICSA Guide to Best Practice for AGMs

The ICSA Guide to Best Practice for Annual General Meetings was published in September 1996 with the endorsement of the NAPF, the ABI and ProShare.

The guide contains 24 elements of best practice, which listed companies in particular are encouraged to follow. These points are supplemented by several other suggestions and recommendations which, although not deemed to qualify for best practice status, were included to stimulate discussion and further development by companies. Many of the points have subsequently been incorporated into the Combined Code (see page 54).

The guide is generally structured to deal with AGM matters in the order in which they arise. Although the guide is written with AGMs in mind many of the points are relevant to general meetings as well.

Checklist

General

- All companies should engage in an active policy of communication with all shareholders.
- Companies should arrange for correspondence from shareholders to receive a full reply from the company secretary, the chairman, another director, or another designated senior executive. In some circumstances it may be appropriate for the response to come from the head of the business division or a particular factory.
- Communications with members should be handled appropriately but sensitively, in accordance with the company's shareholder communications policy.

Before the AGM

- The notice and accompanying documents should be circulated at least 20 working days (excluding weekends and bank holidays) in advance of the meeting.

- The venue for the AGM should be accessible by attendees who have disabilities, and should have facilities for those with poor hearing.
- Companies should ensure that each item of special business included in the notice is accompanied by a full and detailed explanation.
- When proposing directors for election or re-election, it is best practice:
  □ to name them in the notice and form of proxy; and
  □ to provide shareholders with information such as: their age, their relevant experience (not merely a list of other director-ships they hold), the dates that they were first appointed to the board, and details of any board committees to which they belong.
- All the directors to be subject to retirement by rotation.
- All directors should attend the AGM, and all the company's directors should be seated with the chairman, facing the share-holders.

At the AGM

- The chairman should not propose his own election or re-election, or propose any resolution in which he has an interest.
- The resolution to receive or adopt the accounts should be sepa-rate from any resolution to approve the payment of the final dividend recommended by the directors. It is also best practice generally to deal with different items of business by way of sepa-rate resolutions.
- When moving the adoption or receipt of the accounts, the chairman should allow shareholders to raise questions on any item concerning the company's past performance, its results and its intended future performance.
- Boards should provide adequate time for shareholder questions at AGMs.
- Before each resolution is put to the vote, the chairman should:
  □ explain again its effect and purpose and, if necessary, elabo-rate on the information previously provided in the explan-atory circular which accompanied the notice of the meeting;
  □ invite shareholders to speak.
- Where concerns are raised by a shareholder at the AGM and the chairman undertakes to consider them, the shareholder should subsequently be sent a full report of the action taken.
- Except where the company agrees at the outset to absorb all the costs of circulation, shareholder resolutions requisitioned under s.303 of CA 2006 should automatically be accompanied (in any

notice) by another resolution giving shareholders the opportunity to decide whether the company or the requisitionists should bear the relevant costs. If the directors feel that any particular case does not justify the adoption of such a resolution, they should, however, be free to recommend a vote against it.

- When announcing the decision on a poll, the total number of votes cast in favour of, and against, the resolution should be disclosed.
- The chairman should indicate that the number of proxy votes he holds refers to the number lodged with the company (or its registrars) before the meeting and that a number of those who lodged proxies may have attended the meeting and, having heard the debate, decide to vote differently.
- Proxy forms should be worded to allow the proxy to vote or abstain on business which may come before the meeting which was not included in the notice, e.g. amendments and formal motions.
- Companies should provide an updated trading statement at their AGM unless they have recently published a scheduled financial statement.
- At least one of the executive directors of the company should make an oral report, at the AGM, on those areas of the company's operations for which he or she has responsibility.
- Establish procedures for dealing with disturbances at their AGMs.

More information

Manual: Chapter 14.

ICSA Guide to Best Practice for Annual General Meetings.

ICSA Statement on Best Practice: reporting lines for the company secretary

The company secretary is appointed by the board of directors, is an officer of the company and has an important part to play in the corporate governance process.

Boards of directors have a right to expect the company secretary to give impartial advice and to act in the best interests of the company. However, it is incumbent on boards of directors to ensure that company secretaries are in a position to do so, for example by ensuring that they are not subject to the undue influence of one or more of the directors. If the board fails to protect the integrity of the company secretary's position, one of the most effective in-built internal controls available to the company is likely to be seriously undermined. The establishment of appropriate reporting lines for the company secretary will normally be a crucial factor in establishing that protection. It will also be important for non-executive directors to have access to the advice and services of the company secretary and for them to support the company secretary in his or her role.

It is neither practical nor desirable in terms of line management for the company secretary to report on a day-to-day basis to all the directors. However, it is important not to lose sight of the ultimate line of authority when establishing these reporting lines. The company secretary is responsible to the board of directors collectively, rather than to any individual director.

Checklist

- The company secretary is responsible to the board and should be accountable to the board through the chairman on all matters relating to his duties as an officer of the company.
- If the company secretary has other executive or administrative duties, he or she should report to the chief executive or such

other director to whom responsibility for that matter has been delegated by the board.

- The company secretary's salary, share options and benefits should be settled (or at least noted) by the board or the remuneration committee on the recommendation of the chairman or the chief executive.

More information

 Manual: Chapter 12.

ICSA Statement of Best Practice: reporting lines for the company secretary.

Incorporation

The majority of companies are formed on behalf of the ultimate owners by registration agents. It is open to anyone, however, to incorporate a company using the following procedure.

Checklist

- Check the index of company names maintained by the Registrar of Companies to ensure that the proposed name is not the same as or too similar to the name of an existing company. The register can be checked either at Companies House or by accessing the Companies House website (www.companieshouse.gov.uk).   s.66
- Additionally, certain words ('sensitive' words) may require justification or approval by some third party (see page 218).   s.66(4)
- All companies must have at least one subscriber.   s.7
- Private companies must have at least one director and may have a company secretary; public companies must have at least two directors and a company secretary (who can also be a director).   s.154
- The authorised share capital of a public company must be not less than the authorised minimum (£50,000 or euro equivalent).   s.761

Procedure

The following documents must be submitted to the Registrar of Companies: s.7

- The memorandum of association. This must be signed by the subscriber(s) in the presence of at least one witness.
- Articles of association, which again must be signed by the subscriber(s) and the signature(s) witnessed. Alternatively if the model articles are to be adopted without amendment, there is no requirement to file a copy, as the model articles are adopted by default.   ss.9(5), 20, 55
- An application to register a company (form IN01 containing details of the proposed company name, the country of the situation of its registered office, whether the members' liability is limited, and if so whether by shares or guarantee, and whether   ss.9–12

the company is to be a private or public company, the names and addresses of the first director(s), company secretary if there is to be one, and the situation of the registered office. This form must be signed by the first director(s) and secretary, agreeing to act in that capacity, and must also be signed by the subscriber(s) or their agent(s).

- A statement of compliance made by a solicitor or by one of the first directors or secretary confirming that the necessary documents have been properly prepared. *s.13*
- Where appropriate, formal justification of a 'sensitive' name must be submitted with the incorporation papers. *s.66*
- Where appropriate a statement on form NE01 to exempt the company from using the word 'limited' as part of its name. *s.60*
- The registration fee payable (currently £10; same-day fee £50).

Filing requirement

- Form IN01.
- Memorandum and articles of association.
- Filing fee (£10 or £50 for same day incorporation).
- Form NE01 if required.
- Justification for name if required.
- Statement of compliance.

Notes

- By using an appropriate software package, companies can now be incorporated electronically.
- Upon incorporation the Registrar of Companies issues a certificate of incorporation, which shows the date of incorporation, states the status of the company (i.e. private or public) and shows the company's registered number. *s.15*
- A private company is entitled to commence business immediately and there is no requirement for the company to obtain a certificate to commence business.
- The incorporation process for a public company is essentially the same as that for a private company, with the exception that the form of Memorandum and articles of association is different and that the company must have a minimum authorised share capital of £50,000 or euro equivalent and a minimum of two directors and a company secretary.
- Before a public company may commence business or exercise its borrowing powers, it must apply for a trading certificate using form SH50. This certificate will only be issued once the company has a nominal issued capital of at least £50,000 (or euro *s.761* *s.584*

equivalent) with the nominal value each share at least 25 per cent paid-up plus the whole of any premium, if any.

More information

Handbook: Chapter 1. Manual: Chapter 1.
Companies House: GBF1.

Incorporation – completion formalities

Once a company has been incorporated, there are a number of matters that should be formally noted or approved by the directors.

The first directors, company secretary and situation of the registered office will have been determined and shown on application for registration (form IN01), filed with the Registrar of Companies. Particularly where companies are incorporated by registration agents, the first director and secretary will resign and the registered office will be changed immediately following incorporation.

Some or all of the follows matters will require attention.

Checklist

- Appoint director(s) and company secretary, if any, to replace incorporation agents.
- Appoint a managing director or chairman of the board.
- Appoint bankers, including approval of the relevant bank mandate.
- Appoint solicitors to act on behalf of the company.
- Appoint accountants and auditors.
- Set the company's accounting reference date.
- Approve the transfer of the subscriber shares, if appropriate.
- Allot shares in the capital of the company and approve the issue of share certificates.
- Dispense with the need for distinguishing numbers on fully paid shares;.
- Notify the Registrar, if appropriate, of the place where directors' service contracts and the statutory books are situated, if other than at the registered office.
- Some or all of the directors may require service contracts.
- The directors may decide to effect directors' indemnity insurance.
- Consider arrangements regarding PAYE, VAT, insurance and the possible need to register trade marks in the company's name.

- If the company is to have employees, then employer's liability insurance is compulsory.
- Appropriate company headed stationery should be obtained. See page 112.

Procedure

- Convene a directors' meeting, for directors to consider and approve any changes required. Ensure valid quorum present.
- Write up the statutory books to record changes in director(s) and company secretary, transfers or allotment of shares and directors interests.

Filing requirement

- As required forms AP01, AP02, AP03, AD01, SH01, AA01 within 15 days.
- Form SH50 prior to commencing to trade (public companies only).

Notes

- Form AA01, notifying the Registrar of the company's accounting reference date, should be submitted. If this form is not received by the Registrar, the company's first financial year will end on the last day of the month of the anniversary of its incorporation. If a company subsequently decides to have a different accounting reference date, it will be necessary to amend the accounting reference date deemed to have been given to the company, on form AA01.   s.390
- If the company is to adopt a company seal, this should be formally approved by the directors. It is no longer necessary for a company to have a seal, as the company may rely on s.46 of the Companies Act 2006. If the company does rely on this section, documents executed by the directors must be expressed as having been executed on behalf of the company, i.e. 'Executed as a deed this . . . day of . . . 20 . . on behalf of . . . Limited in the presence of . . .'.   s.45

More information

Handbook: Chapter 1. Manual: Chapter 1.
Companies House: GBF1.

Insolvency – administration

Insolvency legislation is complex and outside the scope of this book. However it is appropriate for company secretaries to be aware of the procedures applicable to the appointment of an administrator, and these are detailed below.

A company becomes insolvent when it is unable to pay its debts as they fall due. In circumstances where the directors realise the company will become insolvent, but has not reached that point, they might wish to appoint an administrator to manage the company until it is able to continue, or be sold, or if these are not possible, to be wound up.

Part II EA 2002

Checklist

A company is deemed unable to pay its debts if:

s.123 IA 1986

- it is unable to pay a debt of £750 or more within 21 days of a formal demand in the prescribed form; or
- execution issued on a judgment remains unsatisfied in whole or in part (England and Wales); or
- the court is satisfied that the company is unable to meet its debts as they fall due; or
- the court is satisfied that the value of the company's assets is less than the amount of its liabilities; or
- a charge for payment on an extract decree, extract registered bond or extract registered process has expired without payment (Scotland); or
- a certificate of unenforceability has been granted in respect of judgment (Northern Ireland).

Procedure

- There are three methods of appointing an administrator:
  - □ on application to the court by the company, a majority of its directors, a qualifying floating charge holder, or one or more creditors;
  - □ out-of-court appointment by a qualifying floating charge holder; or

☐ the company or a majority of its directors.

- Once a company is in administration, all business documents issued by it must state the name of the administrator and that the business and affairs of the company are being managed by the administrator.

- While an administration order is in force, the company cannot be wound up and an administrative receiver cannot be appointed or, if previously appointed, they must vacate office. There are restrictions on enforcing any security over the company's property, selling any goods and starting any legal proceedings.

Filing requirement

- Forms [2.6, 2.6b, 2.7, 2.9b, 2.10b, 2,12b] as appropriate

More information

Handbook: Chapter 20. Manual: Chapter 18.
Companies House: GBW1, GBW2 and GBW1(S), and GBW2(S) for Scotland .

The Insolvency Service: www.insolvency.gov.uk/guidanceleaflets/guides.htm.

Insolvency – receivership

Insolvency legislation is complex and outside the scope of this book. However it is appropriate for company secretaries to be aware of the procedures applicable to the appointment of a receiver, and these are detailed below.

An administrative receiver is a receiver or manager of the whole or substantially the whole of a company's property and business, appointed by or on behalf of the holders of debentures of the company secured by a floating charge. An appointee under a fixed charge will normally have no power to manage the business and is, as such, known merely as 'a receiver'.

Receivers are appointed either by the courts or by debenture holders.

Checklist

- Check the deed of appointment and a copy of the debenture (or trust deed) in order to consider the validity of the debenture and the receiver's appointment.

Procedure

Appointment by the court

A court may appoint a receiver on the application of a mortgagee or a debenture holder in the following circumstances:

- where repayment of principal and/or interest is in arrears;
- when the security has become crystallised into a specific charge by the making of a winding-up order or the passing of a resolution to wind up;
- where the security of the mortgagee or the debenture holder is in jeopardy;
- a receiver may also be appointed by the court on the application either of a contributory (i.e. a person liable to contribute to the assets of the company in the event of its being wound up) or of the company. The court will sometimes appoint a receiver and a manager on a short-term basis if the directors are not fulfilling

their functions of management, for instance because of a dispute between them, and pending a general meeting where there has been no governing body. A court will not, however, appoint a receiver if winding-up would be more appropriate.

Appointment by debenture holders

The appointment is made under a deed executed by the debenture holder and is, together with the debenture, evidence of his capacity. The appointment of a receiver usually arises in the following circumstances:

- failure to pay the principal and/or interest in accordance with the terms of the debenture;
- where a borrowing limit has been exceeded and has not been reduced within a specified period;
- a breach of some other provisions in the debenture or trust deed.

Filing requirement

- There are a variety of forms that are required, depending upon which of the two methods of winding up is used. The receiver or proposed receiver will normally arrange filing of the relevant forms and this will not fall to the company secretary.

Notes

- The appointment as receiver or manager must be accepted before the end of the next business day following receipt of the instrument of appointment and shall be deemed to be effective from the time and date the instrument of appointment was received.

More information

Handbook: Chapters 8 and 20.   Manual: Chapter 18.
Companies House: GBW1 and GBW(S) for Scotland.

Insolvency – winding up (liquidation)

Insolvency legislation is complex and outside the scope of this book. However it is appropriate for company secretaries to be aware of the procedures applicable to the appointment of a liquidator, and these are detailed below.

A company becomes insolvent when it is unable to pay its debts as they fall due. Once this stage has been reached, in order to protect the interests of creditors, employees and shareholders, the directors must take steps for the company's affairs to be wound up. Winding up involves the realisation of the company's assets. The process is administered by a licensed insolvency practitioner, who is appointed as liquidator of the company. Winding up is frequently known as liquidation.

Checklist

There are several methods of winding up:

- Members' voluntary winding up: only available where the company is solvent, requiring the directors to give a declaration that the company can meet its debts in full, with interest, during the period of 12 months from the date of commencement of winding up. *ss.89, 90 IA 1986*
- Creditors' voluntary winding up: applicable where a declaration of solvency cannot be given. *s.98 IA 1986*
- Winding up by the courts:
  - by special resolution of the members;
  - on petition of a judgment creditor where a debt of not less than £750 has not been paid within 21 days of a demand in the prescribed form; *s.123 IA 1986*
  - where it is just and equitable that the company be wound up;
  - if the company fails to meet specific statutory requirements, such as minimum number of shareholders. *ss.122, 124*

Procedure

Members' voluntary

- The company's board of directors resolves to make a declaration of solvency, which must embody a statement of assets and liabilities and be made within five weeks immediately before the passing of the resolution to wind up. The declaration has to be filed with the Registrar of Companies within 15 days of the passing of the resolution to wind up.
- The board of directors will also authorise the calling of a general meeting at which a special resolution to wind up will be considered. An ordinary resolution will suffice if the period of life of the company has expired, or on the occurrence of an event on the happening of which the articles provide that the company should be wound up.
- If the resolution is passed, it will be necessary to appoint a liquidator. This may be done by an ordinary resolution of the company.
- The resolution to wind up, signed by the chairman of the meeting, should be published in the *London Gazette* or the *Edinburgh Gazette*, as appropriate, within 14 days of being passed. The resolution and all documents for publication in each *Gazette* must be authenticated by a solicitor or a member of an established body of accountants or secretaries. The resolution to wind up must also be filed within 15 days with the Registrar of Companies.
- The liquidator must, within 14 days of his or her appointment, advertise his appointment in each *Gazette* and give notice to the Registrar of Companies on form G600.

Creditors' voluntary

- A meeting of the board of directors will authorise the calling of a general meeting to consider an ordinary resolution that the company, by reason of its liabilities, cannot continue and that it is advisable to wind up.
- A meeting of the creditors should be called by the company to be held within 14 days of the members' meeting to consider the resolution to wind up. At least seven days' notice of the meeting must be given to the creditors. Notice of the creditors' meeting should be advertised in the appropriate *Gazette* and two local newspapers.
- The notice must state either:
  - □ the name and address of the insolvency practitioner who will give such information to the creditors before the meeting takes place as they may reasonably require; or

- □ a place in the principal area of business of the company where a list of names and addresses of the company's creditors will be available for inspection without charge.
- The creditors' meeting will be presided over by one of the directors, who should prepare a statement of affairs in the prescribed form, verified by affidavit, to be laid before the creditors' meeting.
- At the general meeting an ordinary resolution is passed to wind up and an ordinary resolution is passed to nominate the liquidator.
- At the creditors' meeting, which must be attended by the proposed liquidator, the directors may answer questions put to them by the creditors concerning the administration of the company, although there is no legal requirement for them to do so.
- The liquidator shall be the person nominated by the creditors or, where no other person has been so nominated, the person (if any) nominated by the company. Where a different person is nominated by the creditors, any member or creditor of the company may apply to the court within seven days for an order that the members' nomination shall remain liquidator instead of, or jointly with, the creditors' nomination, or that some other person be appointed.

By the court

- When the court makes a winding-up order, the Official Receiver becomes the liquidator.
- The Official Receiver may require officers of the company or other persons as specified to prepare, swear and submit a statement of affairs within 21 days.
- Separate meetings of creditors and contributories may be summoned by the Official Receiver at his discretion for the appointment of some other person to be liquidator of the company. Contributions are defined by the IA s.79 but are usually synonymous with the term 'members'. The Official Receiver remains liquidator if another person is not appointed. The Official Receiver must summon a meeting for the appointment of another liquidator if one-quarter in value of the creditors requisition him to do so on IR Form No. 4.21, in accordance with the IA s.136(5)(c) and IR 4.57.
- The court may make any appointment or order to give effect to the wishes of the meetings or make any other order that it may think fit.
- The creditors and contributories may nominate as liquidator any

person who is qualified to act as an insolvency practitioner and in the absence of a nomination by the creditors the contributories' nominee (if any) will be the liquidator.

■ At any time the Official Receiver may apply to the Secretary of State for the appointment of a liquidator in his place. Any such liquidator must send notice of his appointment as the court may direct.

Filing requirement

■ There are a variety of forms that are required depending upon which of the three methods of winding up is used. The liquidator or proposed liquidator will normally arrange filing of the relevant forms and this will not fall to the company secretary.

Notes

■ On the appointment of a liquidator, all the powers of the directors cease.
■ The creditors have the power to appoint a liquidation committee, which may sanction the continuation of some of the directors powers.
■ The remuneration of the liquidator is fixed by the liquidation committee or, if there is no committee, by the creditors, failing which it is based on the scales applicable to the Official Receiver under IR 19.

More information

Handbook: Chapters 8 and 20. Manual: Chapter 19.
Companies House: GBW1 and GBW2, and GBW1(S) and GBW2(S) for Scotland.

The Insolvency Service www.insolvency.gov.uk/guidanceleaflets/guides.htm.

Inspection of registers and other documents

The Act requires that every company keep various registers, and stipulates where they must be held and provisions regarding their inspection, other than the register of directors' residential addresses. Inspection of all the registers is free to members, and in the case of the register of charges, free to creditors. Anyone else may be required to pay a fee.

Checklist

- The general position is that all the registers must be kept at and be available for inspection either at the registered office or a place of inspection. s.1136
- The following registers and documents must be available for inspection:
  - □ section 114 (register of members);
  - □ section 162 (register of directors);
  - □ section 228 (directors' service contracts);
  - □ section 237 (directors' indemnities);
  - □ section 275 (register of secretaries);
  - □ section 358 (records of resolutions etc);
  - □ section 702 (contracts relating to purchase of own shares);
  - □ section 720 (documents relating to redemption or purchase of own shares out of capital by private company);
  - □ section 743 (register of debenture holders);
  - □ section 805 (report to members of outcome of investigation by public company into interests in its shares);
  - □ section 809 (register of interests in shares disclosed to public company);
  - □ section 877 (instruments creating charges and register of charges: England and Wales);
  - □ section 892 (instruments creating charges and register of charges: Scotland).

Filing requirement

■ Forms AD02, AD03, AD04 as required.

Notes

■ The registers and other documents of a public company must be available for inspection for at least two hours between 9.00 a.m. and 5.00 p.m. on business days.

reg.5
SI 2008/3006

■ The registers and other documents of a private company must be available for inspection for at least two hours between 9.00 a.m. and 3.00 p.m. on business days and the company must be given two days' notice of inspection where such request is made during the notice period of a meeting or during the circulation period of a written resolution and ten days' notice at all other times.

reg.4
SI 2008/3009

Fees payable

■ The company is obliged to provide copies of certain registers and documents upon payment of a fee.

Fees in respect of inspection of registers by non-members

■ The fee relates to the inspection of the registers of: members, register of interests in shares and register of debenture holders.
■ £3.50 per hour or part thereof during which the register(s) is (are) inspected.

Fees for provision of copies of entries in registers and copies of reports

■ The fees for copies of the registers of: debentures, register of interests in voting shares and registers of debenture holders or members are:
  □ £1.00 for the first five entries;
  □ £30.00 for the next 95 entries or part thereof;
  □ £30.00 for the next 900 entries or part thereof;
  □ £30.00 for the next 99,000 entries or part thereof;
  □ £30 for the remainder of the entries in the register.
■ Fees for provision of copies of trust deeds, service contracts, and minutes: 10 pence per 500 words or part thereof.

More information

📕 Handbook: Chapter 12. 📓 Manual: Chapter 5.

Joint shareholders

Occasionally, shares will be issued or transferred jointly to two or more persons. The articles of association of the company may place a limit on the number of holders. Under Stock Exchange and Plus market rules, listed, AIM and PLUS public companies must allow for a minimum of four joint holders.

Listed below are suggested solutions to particular problems or queries that can arise, in relation to joint holdings.

Joint holders may request that the shares registered in their names be split into two or more accounts, with the holders' names being shown in a different order. Such requests are commonly dealt with without the need for a stock transfer form, provided the request is in writing and signed by all the joint holders. Additionally, it will be necessary for the share certificate to be returned for cancellation and new certificates issued. For ease of administration, however, companies may prefer to deal with such requests by designation of accounts rather than by rearranging the order of the names.

Occasionally, the joint holders will request that the order of the names on the joint account be changed and again most companies will process this without the need for a formal stock transfer form, provided the request is in writing, signed by all the joint holders and includes confirmation that no sale or disposition has taken place. Again, the share certificate should be returned for cancellation. All communications for the shareholders will be sent to the first-named of the joint holders.

The joint holders may request that communications be sent to someone other than the first-named; however, for administrative reasons this may be impractical. Additionally, the articles of association may prohibit such a request.

More information

Handbook: Chapter 4. Manual: Chapters 5, 6, 7 and 14.

Joint shareholders – death of one shareholder

When a joint shareholder dies, the surviving holder or holders in whose name or names the shares are registered become the beneficiaries of the share. There is no need for a stock transfer form to be completed.

The company will require sight of the death certificate or an authenticated copy of it. The register of members should be amended to note the death of one holder.

The company may require a new dividend mandate to be given.

The share certificate may be either endorsed or cancelled and a new certificate issued.

It is important to establish the correct address for the surviving joint shareholder(s), as if it is the first-named holder that has died, the address details for the next first-named holder may be several years old.

Checklist
- Amend register of members.
- Endorse or issue a replacement share certificate. (Replacement is often more appropriate, as otherwise the surviving joint holders will be reminded of the deceased joint holder whenever the records are reviewed.)

Procedure
- Note death details on register of members.
- Confirm correspondence address for surviving joint holder(s)

Filing requirement
- None.

More information
Handbook: Chapter 4. Manual: Chapters 5 and 6.

Loan stock

The procedure for the issue of loan stock, and thereafter the payment of any interest and the holding of meetings, are, subject to a trust deed creating the loan stock, similar to the procedures for the issue, declaration of dividend and requirements for meetings of ordinary shares.

The most important difference is that the loan stock will be created by a trust deed setting out the rights attaching to the stock.

Checklist

- Check the articles to ensure directors have authority to create loan stock.
- The trust deed should cover the following points:
  - □ Details of the stock, aggregate amount of stock, the units in which it may be issued or transferred and details of repayment and interest.
  - □ Provisions creating a charge over the company's assets and stipulating under what circumstances the security is enforceable.
  - □ The powers of the trustee. In particular the trustee is usually instructed to concur with the company in all dealings relating to the charged assets.
  - □ Provisions stipulating that no additional charges can be created ranking ahead of the stock without written consent of the loan stockholders.
  - □ Schedules detailing the repayment conditions, transfer conditions, regulations for meetings and the form of stock certificate.

Procedure

- Convene a directors' meeting to approve the creation of the loan stock deed and issue of loan stock. Ensure valid quorum present.
- Enter details in register of loan stock (if kept).
- Issue appropriate loan stock certificates.

Filing requirement

- None unless secured, in which case the charge needs to be registered (see page 193).

Notes

- The company is not required by statute to keep a register of loan stock holders. However; for practical reasons this is usually done and, in such circumstances, the register of loan stock holders should be in the same form as the register of members.
- Stock is issued by resolution of the directors as with the share capital, although there is no requirement to file a return with the Registrar of Companies.

More information

Handbook: Chapter 4. Manual: Chapters 2 and 9.

Loan stock – convertible

It is common for the terms of issue of loan stock (more usually **unsecured** loan stock) to include provisions for the loan stock to be converted into share capital. Usually the loan stock will be convertible into equity shares, although the stock may be convertible into another class of shares.

Checklist

■ Ensure there is no restriction on the number of shares that may be allotted without seeking the consent of members (see page 143).
■ Ensure directors have authority to issue shares.   ss.549(1)

Procedure

■ Convene a directors' meeting to consider the conversion of the stock, whether in full or in part. Ensure valid quorum present. The precise procedures to be followed will be stipulated in the loan stock deed.
■ The company secretary should prepare a circular letter to the holders giving details of the conversion procedure, including a form of nomination and acceptance for their use. A form of nomination is necessary in the event that any particular stockholder requires the shares to be registered in another person's name.
■ As the completed notices of conversion and forms of nomination and acceptance are received, these should be checked against the register of stockholders to ensure that the details are correct. The loan stock certificates should be returned for cancellation. Once the period for conversion has elapsed, a list of shares to be issued should be compiled and the directors should formally allot the shares. A return of allotments should be submitted to the registrar of companies within 15 days.
■ Share certificates evidencing the shares issued should be prepared and issued to the shareholders within two months of the date of allotment.

- The register of members should be amended to record the shares now issued, and the register of loan stock should be amended to show the loan stock that has been cancelled.
- Where the conversion of the loan stock is only for part of the stock, a balancing loan stock certificate should be issued.

Filing requirement

- Form SH01 within 15 days.

More information

Handbook: Chapter 4. Manual: Chapters 2 and 9.

Loan stock – unsecured

Unsecured loan stock carries a greater risk for investors than secured loan stock, and as a result will usually attract a higher rate of interest. Additionally, as an added incentive, the holders may be given options to acquire equity capital in the future, usually by conversion of the unsecured loan stock into equity shares, rather than by repayment of the loan. As with secured loan stock, the issue of unsecured loan stock and the rights and privileges attaching to the stock are governed by a trust deed

Checklist

- Check the articles to ensure directors have authority to create loan stock.
- The trust deed should cover the following points:
  - details of the terms of issue, amounts payable on the stock and, where these are payable by more than one instalment, dates and terms of the instalments, details of the repayment or redemption of the stock and interest payments, and any rights of conversion or options on shares in the capital of the company;
  - restrictions on further issues of unsecured loan stock without the approval of the existing loan stockholders;
  - restriction on the borrowing powers of the company without prior approval;
  - restrictions on the disposal by the company of certain assets or other sale agreements without prior approval;
  - guarantees by the company that it will maintain sufficient unissued share capital to satisfy any conversion or option rights given to the loan stockholders;
  - the actions open to the stockholders in the event of non-payment of interest or non-redemption of the stock on the due date;
  - details of the trustees to the issue and of any remuneration payable;
  - schedules containing the form of stock certificate, option certificates, notices of redemption and detailed conditions

concerning the redemption, whether in whole or in part, and any conversion rights or options given to the holders.

Procedure

- Convene a directors' meeting to approve the creation of the loan stock deed and issue of loan stock. Ensure valid quorum present.
- Enter details in register of loan stock (if kept).
- Issue appropriate loan stock certificates.

Filing requirement

- None.

Notes

- The procedures to be followed for the issue or repayment of unsecured loan stock are the same as for loan stock (see page 139).
- The conversion procedure, where relevant, is the same as for convertible loan stock (see page 141).

More information

Handbook: Chapter 4. Manual: Chapters 2 and 9.

Loans to directors

Except under specified circumstances, companies are not permitted to make loans, or quasi-loans nor enter into credit arrangements with their directors, directors of their holding company or persons connected to them, unless the transaction has been approved by ordinary resolution of the members. Where the director concerned is a director of the holding company, the transaction must be approved by members of the holding company.

ss.197–203

Approval is not required where funds are being made available to meet expenditure made or to be made for the purposes of the company or to enable the director to perform their duties as a director of the company.

s.204

Checklist

The following transactions do not require approval from members:

- Quasi-loans of up to £10,000, where repayment is required within two months.
- Loans to director of company or holding company not exceeding £10,000.
- Loans to director by relevant company in ordinary course of business on an arm's-length, commercial basis. Where a loan is proposed for the purchase of a home, this must be for the director's only or main residence or for the improvement of such a residence.
- Loans to cover out-of-pocket expenses to be incurred in performance of duties, not exceeding £50,000.

s.207
s.207
s.209

Procedure

- Check if proposed loan falls within one of the permitted exceptions.
- Convene a directors' meeting to consider the making of a loan or credit arrangement to a director. Ensure valid quorum present.
- Ensure director notifies interest in proceedings (see page 86).
- Convene general meeting to approve ordinary resolution or, if a private company, circulate a written resolution.

Filing requirement

■ None.

More information

Handbook: Chapter 2. Manual: Chapters 11 and 16.

Memorandum of association

From 1 October 2009 the content of the memorandum of association is changing such that it will now only contain details of the subscribers.

s.8

To form a company, one or more persons must subscribe to a memorandum of association.

For an existing company, any other provisions set out in their memorandum will be deemed to form part of their articles of association.

Filing requirement

■ On incorporation, a copy of the memorandum of association is required to be filed with the other incorporation documents.

s.9

Minutes

Directors are required to ensure that minutes are kept of all direc-   ss.248, 355
tors', shareholders' and class meetings and of members' resolutions
approved otherwise than at a general or class meeting, and that
these are kept in appropriate minute books.

Checklist

- Minutes should state the name of the company, the place, date
  and time of the meeting.
- If a list of attendees is not included or attached to the minutes,
  the minutes should state that a quorum was present.
- The minutes should record decisions reached by the meeting,
  together with sufficient detail of the discussions to enable the
  sense of the meeting to be established.
- Any specific disagreement by a director with a particular resolution or course of action should be recorded.

Procedure

- It is normally the company secretary who takes the minutes of
  proceedings and who prepares the first draft.
- The draft minutes are circulated to those attending for
  comments.
- Although not a requirement, it is useful for the chairman to sign
  the agreed minutes.
- Signed minutes are evidence of the discussions and agreement   s.249
  reached.

Filing requirement

- None.

Notes

- When draft minutes are circulated for comments, care must be
  taken to ensure that any suggested amendments do not reflect
  what a speaker meant to say, rather than what was actually said.

- Directors are entitled to have access to directors' minutes.
- Shareholders may inspect the minutes of shareholder meetings   s.358
  or, on payment of a prescribed fee, may request copies of shareholder minutes to be sent to them, within seven days. Shareholders have no right to view minutes of the directors' meetings.
- Minutes of directors' and shareholder meetings must be kept for   ss.248(2),
  at least ten years from the date of the meeting.   355(2)

More information

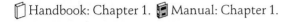Handbook: Chapter 1. Manual: Chapter 1.

Name change

A company may change its name by special resolution of the members or by other means provided for in its articles of association.

s.77(1)

Certain words are deemed to be 'sensitive' and require justification or due authority before the Registrar of Companies will allow their use (see page 218).

ss.55–57, 1193–1198

Checklist

- Check that the proposed name is available by checking the register of company names (www.companieshouse.gov.uk).

  s.66
  ss.1080, 1085

- The name of a private company must end with either 'limited' or 'ltd', or the Welsh equivalents 'cyfyngedig' or 'cyf'. Certain guarantee or non-profit-making companies and charitable companies are exempt from this provision if they meet qualifying criteria or are community interest companies.

  s.60–62
  s.33 C(AICE)A 2004

- The name of a public company must end with either 'public limited company' or 'plc', or the Welsh equivalents 'cwmni cyfngedig cyhoeddus' or 'ccc'. Community interest companies are not subject to this provision.

  s.58
  s 33 C(AICE)A 2004

- Does the name contain only permitted characters?

  s.57

- Is the name misleading or does it contain sensitive words or expressions?

  ss.54–56, 65

- Although not a legal requirement, it is advisable to check the proposed names against the trade mark registry and registered internet domain names so as to limit the possibility of objections being raised with the company names adjudicator by third parties with goodwill in the name.

  s.69

Procedure

- Convene a directors' meeting to recommend appropriate special resolution to members and to convene a general meeting or circulate a written resolution as appropriate. Alternatively use any alternative procedure contained in the company's articles of association. Ensure valid quorum present.
- Where a general meeting is to be held, issue notice, signed by

director or company secretary, on 14 clear days' notice for members to consider resolution.

- Enclose with the notice a form of proxy if desired. Listed companies must enclose a two-way form of proxy (see page 176).
- If the meeting is to be convened on short notice, the company secretary should arrange for agreement to short notice to be signed by each of the members.
- Hold general meeting. Ensure valid quorum is present. Resolution put to vote either by show of hands or by poll and to be passed by appropriate majority (special resolution by 75 per cent majority).
- Amend articles of association, if these contain a company name clause.
- Alternatively the directors may be directed by the Secretary of State to change the name of the company, in which case a resolution of shareholders is not required.

ss.64, 1033

Filing requirement

- Copy of change of resolution within 15 days.
- Notice of change of name on form NM01, NM02, NM04 or NM05, as appropriate.
- Filing fee £10 (same-day fee £50).
- Justification for sensitive word(s) if required.
- Amended copy of articles of association, if required.

ss.78(1), 79(1)

s.26

Notes

- The change of name only takes effect when the Registrar issues a revised certificate of incorporation.
- Once the Registrar has issued the revised certificate of incorporation, it will be necessary to obtain new headed stationery, amend email and website disclosures, and order a new company seal, where the company has a seal.
- Arrange for the name of the company's bank accounts to be changed and for the company's articles of association to be amended and reprinted.
- Notify the company's suppliers and customers of the change of name (e.g. British Telecom), HM Revenue & Customs for corporation tax, PAYE and VAT, pension scheme, title deeds, trade mark registrations, data protection registration, insurers, etc. Signs at the company's premises or on the company's cars, vans and lorries will also require amendment.
- Listed, AIM and PLUS companies must make appropriate market disclosures.

s.80

s.82

More information

📓 Handbook: Chapters 2 and 12. 📕 Manual: Chapters 10, 13 and 14.
© Handbook: Chapters 2 and 12.

Notice periods

Although directors' meetings may be held on 'reasonable' notice, there are strict rules governing the notice periods for shareholders' meetings.

Checklist

- Annual general meeting of a public company: 21 days   s.307(2)(a)
- General meeting of a public company: 14 days   s.307(2)(b)
- General meeting of a private company: 14 days   s.307(1)

Resolutions requiring special notice

- Notice to company of intention to put resolution: 28 days   s.312

Procedure

- Convene a directors' meeting to recommend appropriate resolution(s) to members and to convene a general meeting. Ensure valid quorum present.
- Issue notice either in hard copy, in electronic form or by means of a website.
- Issue with the notice a form of proxy if desired. Listed companies   s.308
  must enclose a two-way form of proxy (see page 176).
- Consider whether class meeting(s) also required.
- If the meeting is to be convened on short notice, the company secretary should arrange for agreement to short notice to be signed by each of the shareholders.

Filing requirement

- None.

Notes

- Notices convening an annual general meeting of a public company must state that the meeting is to be an annual general meeting.

- Period of notice is stated in 'clear' days. The articles should be consulted to ascertain what constitutes 'clear' days for the particular company. For example, the company's articles may state that the day of receipt must be classed as 48 hours, and not 24 hours after posting.
- Under the Combined Code, listed companies should give 20 working days' notice of their AGM.
- Companies formed prior to 1 October 2009 must take great care to check their articles, as these are very likely to contain the notice periods under the former Companies Act, which are longer in certain circumstances.

More information

☐ Handbook: Chapter 1. ☐ Manual: Chapter 1.

Notice – special

Certain resolutions require that 28 days' special notice of the intention to put that resolution be given to the company. Other than where resolutions are proposed by shareholders, this special notice would be given by a director or the company secretary.

s.312

Checklist

The following resolutions require special notice to be given to the company.

- Removal of a director (see page 92).   s.168
- Removal of an auditors or appointment as auditors of someone   s.511
  other than the retiring auditors (see page 38).
- Appointment of auditors to fill casual vacancy or re-   s.515
  appointment of auditors following appointment by directors to
  fill casual vacancy (see pages 34 and 36).

Procedure

- Letter to the company stating the intention to propose appro-   s.312
  priate resolution and stating that special notice is being given
  must be lodged at the company's registered office at least 28 days
  prior to the meeting.
- The company must, where practical, give its members notice of   s.312(2)
  any such resolution in the same manner and at the same time as
  it gives notice of the meeting. If that is not possible it must give   s.312(3)
  at least 14 days' notice by newspaper advertisement or such
  other method provided in its articles.
- If the resolution relates to the proposed removal of a director, a
  copy of the special notice must be sent as soon as possible to the
  director concerned.

Filing requirement

- None.

Notes

- If after special notice has been given the meeting is convened for a date sooner than 28 days, notice is deemed properly given although not within the time required.   s.312(4)

More information

Handbook: Chapter 9. Manual: Chapter 14.

Notices – content

Checklist

Notices should contain the following information:

- Company name.
- Date and time of meeting.   s.311(1)(a)
- Place of meeting.   s.311(1)(b)
- General nature of business to be transacted.   s.311(2)
- Notice of a public company AGM must state that the meeting is   s.337(1) to be an AGM.
- Where a special resolution is to be proposed, the notice must   s.283(6) state that the resolution is to be proposed as a special resolution and contain the text of the resolution.
- For listed, AIM and PLUS companies, resolutions on substantially different matters should be separate resolutions and not bundled.
- Public companies must consider the appointment or re-appoint-   s.160 ment of directors as separate resolutions.
- Statement that members may appoint proxies who need not   s.325 themselves be members.
- Companies whose shares are settled in Crest will usually state a   s.41 USR 1985 date not more than 48 hours before the meeting as the cut-off for registrations to determine entitlement to attend and vote. In practice, due to the difficulty in establishing the entitlement to attend part-way through a trading day, the cut-off is usually stated as being the holdings at the close of business on the pre-penultimate day before the day of the meeting.

Procedure

- Convene a directors' meeting to recommend appropriate resolution(s) to members and to convene a general meeting. Ensure valid quorum present.
- Issue notice either in hard copy, in electronic form or by means   s.308 of a website.
- Issue with the notice a form of proxy if desired. Listed companies must enclose a two-way form of proxy (see page 176).

- Consider whether class meeting(s) also required.
- If the meeting is to be convened on short notice, the company secretary should arrange for agreement to short notice to be signed by each of the shareholders.

Filing requirement

- None.

More information

Handbook: Chapter 9. Manual: Chapter 14.

Overseas company

The provisions relating to overseas companies are contained in ss.1044–1059 and the Overseas Companies Regulations 2009 ('OCR').

Any overseas company which opens a UK establishment must register certain particulars with the Registrar of Companies. A UK establishment is either a branch within the meaning of the eleventh Company Law Directive, or a place of business that is not a branch.

OCR reg.3

The previous distinction and different filing regimes for branches and places of business have been replaced by one registration regime.

If an overseas company has already registered details for another UK establishment, details applicable to both registrations need not be repeated but may be referred to.

OCR reg.3(2)

Checklist

- If the parent company's incorporation documents are not in English, a certified translation will be required.
- If another UK establishment has been registered, details of that registration will be required.

Procedure

Complete form OS IN01 containing the following information:

OCR reg.5

- the company's registered name;
- its legal form (public, private, etc.);
- if registered in its country of incorporation, its registered number and the identity of the register;
- details of directors and secretary, or their equivalent;
- the authority of the directors to represent the company and their capacity to bind the company in dealings with third parties, together with a statement of whether this authority may be exercised solely or jointly with other directors;
- whether the company is a credit or financial institution.

If the overseas company is not incorporated in a member state of the European Union, the following additional information must be provided:

OCR reg.5(2)

- the legislation under which the company was incorporated must be stated;
- the address of the principal place of business, the country of incorporation, the objects of the company and the amount of its issued share capital;
- the accounting reference date and time allowed for filing of accounts available for public inspection (required if the company wishes to take advantage of the right to file in the UK accounts prepared and disclosed in its country of incorporation).

In respect of the UK establishment the following information should be registered:

OCR reg.6

- the address of the establishment;
- the date on which it was opened;
- the business carried on;
- the establishment's trading name if different from the company's registered name;
- the name and service address of all persons resident in the UK authorised to accept service on behalf of the company in respect of that establishment;
- the name and address of all persons authorised to represent the company as permanent representatives for the business of that establishment;
- the authority of the permanent representatives to contract on behalf of the establishment and whether they may exercise such authority solely or if jointly the name of the person(s);
- A statement of how the company intends to meet its obligations relating to accounts and whether those will be met by the establishment being registered or by another UK establishment.

OCR reg.7

Filing requirement

- Form OS IN01.
- A certified copy of the company's constitutional documents.
- A copy of the latest set of audited accounts required to be published by parent law.

(If these documents have been previously filed by another UK establishment, they may be referred to rather than filed again.)

- Registration fee.

Notes

- The constitutional document need only be submitted once and must be referred to for other branch registrations.
- Any alterations to the constitutional documents must be notified on the appropriate form. OCR reg.12
- Each overseas company with a UK establishment must register its annual report and accounts (see page 16). OCR reg.17
- A UK establishment owning property over which charges have been given is required to register details with the Registrar. OCR regs 46, 47
- Every UK establishment of an overseas company shall state the registered branch number and the place of registration of the branch on its headed paper, invoices, etc. If the overseas company is not from an EU member state, the following additional information must be stated: OCR regs 78–86 / OCR reg.83
  - □ the identity of the register and its country of incorporation;
  - □ its registered number, if any;
  - □ the legal form of the company;
  - □ if the liability of its members is limited, that fact;
  - □ the location of its registered office or principal place of business; and
  - □ whether it is in liquidation or any other form of insolvency.
- Where an overseas company which has UK establishment(s) is being wound up it must, within 14 days of the commencement of the winding-up, give details of its name, particulars of the winding-up and the date upon which the winding-up is or will be effective. Within 14 days of appointment the liquidator must notify his or her name and address, the date of his or her appointment and a description of his or her powers. Following the termination of the winding-up for whatever reason, the liquidator must file details of the termination within 14 days. Details must be given for each UK establishment, although one return may be made provided the registered numbers of each UK establishment are stated on the return. OCR reg.56

More information

 Handbook: Chapter 21. Manual: Chapters 1, 5, 6, 10 and 16.
 Companies House: GBO1.

Polls

The rules governing the demanding of a poll will be laid down in the company's articles, or in the appropriate model articles if the company has not adopted its own articles. The provisions of ss.321 and 322 must be considered, however, when drafting a company's articles covering voting on a poll, since by those sections certain provisions are rendered void.

The checklists and procedures set out below are based upon the relevant model articles set out in SI 2009/3229.

Private companies – Sch.1 SI 2009/3229

Checklist

- Check articles to see if model articles provisions adopted.
- Has the demand for a poll been validly made: reg.45(1)
  - ☐ in advance of the general meeting; or
  - ☐ at the meeting on or before the declaration of the result on a show of hands?
- Where model article provisions adopted, a poll may be demanded by the following: reg.45 (2)
  - ☐ the chairman;
  - ☐ the directors;
  - ☐ at least two persons having the right to vote at the meeting;
  - ☐ one or more persons representing not less than one-tenth of the total voting rights of all the members having the right to vote at the meeting.
- Demand for a poll may only be withdrawn if the poll has not taken place and the chairman agrees.   reg.45(3)
- The poll must be taken immediately in such manner as the chairman directs.   reg.45 (4)

Public companies – Sch.3 SI 2009/3229

Checklist

- Check articles to see if model articles provisions adopted.

- Has the demand for a poll been validly made: reg.36(1)
  - □ in advance of the general meeting; or
  - □ at the meeting on or before the declaration of the result on a show of hands.
- Where model article provisions adopted, a poll may be demanded   reg.36(2)
  by the following:
  - □ the chairman;
  - □ the directors;
  - □ at least two persons having the right to vote at the meeting;
  - □ one or more persons representing not less than one-tenth of the total voting rights of all the members having the right to vote at the meeting;
- Demand for a poll may only be withdrawn if the poll has not   reg.36(3)
  taken place and the chairman agrees.
- The poll may be taken in such manner as the chairman directs,   reg.37(1,(5))
  but must be taken within 30 days.
- The chairman may appoint scruntineers, who need not be   reg.37(2)
  members, and may decide how, where and when the results will
  be declared.
- Polls on the election of a chairman or adjournment of the   reg.37(4)
  meeting must be taken immediately.
- No notice need be given if the time and place are announced at   reg.37(7),(8)
  the meeting; otherwise seven days' notice is required.

Quoted companies

- There are additional provisions which quoted companies must
  adhere to.
- A quoted company must publish on a website the results of any   s.341
  poll votes, including date of the meeting, text of the resolution
  and the number of votes cast in favour of and against the resolution.
- Members representing ay least 5 per cent of the total voting   s.342
  rights or 100 members or more may request an independent
  report on a poll taken or to be taken at a general meeting. The
  request may be in hard copy or in electronic form, must identify
  the poll(s) to which it relates, be authenticated by all those
  members requesting it and must be received by the company not
  later than one week after the date the poll is taken.
- Where an independent assessor has been appointed the company   s.351
  must publish on a website details of the appointment, the iden-
  tity of the assessor, the text of the resolution(s) and a copy of the
  independents assessors report.

Procedure

- An announcement should be drafted for the chairman, which can be read out if a poll is demanded, to inform members of the procedure to be followed, or, if the poll is to take place at a later date, of the date and time for the taking of the poll and the procedure to be followed.
- It may be appropriate for the chairman to suggest that since proxies already lodged are overwhelmingly in favour of the resolution, the person or persons requesting the poll may decide to withdraw their demand.
- If the demand for a poll is not withdrawn, the validity of the demand should be checked by confirming that those who have demanded it are, in fact, members or proxies or, for example, if only one member is demanding it, that he or she holds not less than one-tenth of the total voting rights. It is usually the scrutineers' responsibility to check the validity of the demand for the poll.
- If the scrutineers advise that the poll has not been properly demanded, the chairman will make a statement to this effect and the meeting will usually proceed to its next business after having put the matter on which the poll was requested to the vote by a show of hands (if this had not already been done at the time the poll was demanded). Polls on procedural resolutions should take place immediately.
- If the demand for the poll is valid and is not withdrawn, the chairman will advise the meeting to this effect. If the chairman did not advise the meeting as to the proxy position when the poll was first demanded, this could now be done. Assuming the poll is still not withdrawn, the chairman will read the statement announcing the time for holding of the poll, e.g. either immediately, at the conclusion of the meeting or at a later date. It is usual practice for the poll to be held at the end of the meeting and for it to be kept open for one hour. The meeting then proceeds to its next business until the conclusion of the business of the meeting.
- At the end of the meeting the chairman declares the meeting closed and informs the members as to the procedure for the conduct of the poll. He explains that those who have appointed a proxy need not complete a ballot paper unless they wished to alter their vote.
- Stewards then distribute ballot papers to those present. These are collected by staff after completion by the members and proxy holders and handed to the scrutineers.
- The scrutineers, especially if they are the company's auditors,

have their own instructions with regard to the checking of the ballot papers, verification of the holdings, and preparation of a report and final certificate of the result of the poll. This is handed to the chairman, who then declares the results of the poll. In the case of a listed company, or a company whose shares are traded on AIM or PLUS the result of the poll is notified to the Stock Exchange or PLUS as appropriate.

Filing requirement

- None.

Notes

- As procedures can vary from company to company, it is essential that the articles of association are checked to ensure the correct procedure is followed.
- In order for a demand for a poll to be valid, it must be called for before or immediately on the declaration by the chairman of the result of the vote on a show of hands.

More information

Handbook: Chapter 9. Manual: Chapter 14.

Power of attorney – corporate

A corporate power of attorney is an appointment by a company of a person or persons to act on its behalf as set out in the document creating the power of attorney. Attorneys are usually appointed by companies to act on their behalf overseas, although an attorney may be appointed within the UK.

The Powers of Attorney Act 1971 sets out a short form of power of attorney, which may be used to confer wide powers on the attorney. A corporate power of attorney is more likely to be for a specific purpose and would therefore be in a longer form, setting out the precise details of the powers of attorney.

The power of attorney need not be given under seal, provided it is stated as being executed as a deed on behalf of the company.

The directors' authority to delegate their authority to an attorney is contained in the articles of association.

reg.5(b)
Schs.1 and 3
SI 2009/3229

Checklist

■ Check the articles of association to ensure directors' may delegate their authority to an attorney.

Procedure

■ Convene a directors' meeting to approve the terms of the attorney's appointment. Ensure valid quorum present.
■ The document creating the power of attorney to be executed in accordance with the articles of association, usually any two directors, one director and the company secretary, or by a sole director duly witnessed.
■ Any changes required to be made to an existing power of attorney will require a variation to the original agreement.

Filing requirement

■ None.

More information

📕 Handbook: Chapter 8. 📓 Manual: Chapter 6.

Power of attorney – member

Individuals may give a power of attorney either general or specific under the provisions of the Powers of Attorney Act 1971, or a lasting power of attorney under the Mental Capacity Act 2005.

Checklist

- The document received for registration must be the original document, bearing a stamp duty impression if granted prior to 26 March 1985, or an authenticated copy of it.
- Care must be taken to ensure that the person granting the power of attorney is indeed a member of the company and holds the appropriate number of shares. It may be that the power of attorney is being granted by a member who has only recently acquired shares either by allotment, renunciation of bonus or rights issue or by transfer.

Procedure

Where a power of attorney is received for registration, the following procedure should be followed:

- The company should retain a copy of the power of attorney for its records.
- The terms of the power of attorney must be checked to see whether one attorney is being appointed, or more than one. In the case of more than one attorney, it will be necessary to check whether one attorney acting on his or her own has power to effect transfers, or whether all attorneys must act together.
- The power of attorney may change the registered address for the shareholder and the matter of to whom any future dividends must be made.
- If the power of attorney is in order, the company's registration stamp should be affixed to the original document and returned to the person giving the power of attorney.
- On every occasion that documents are executed by the attorney, this should be cross-referenced with the copy of the power of attorney retained by the company to ensure that the terms of the power of attorney have been complied with.

- Neither the name in the register of members nor the original share certificate requires amendment since the beneficial owner is not changing and, indeed, as the register of members is a public document, the appointment of a power of attorney should not be noted on it.
- A power of attorney can be revoked or changed by the person giving the power of attorney at any time or, alternatively, the power of attorney may be given for a specific occasion or for a specific length of time.

Filing requirement

- None.

More information

Handbook: Chapter 8. Manual: Chapter 6.

Pre-emption rights – allotment

Any new equity securities (ordinary shares or rights to convert securities into or subscribe for ordinary shares) to be issued by a company must first be offered to existing members in proportion to the number of shares they already hold. An ordinary share is defined as a share without restriction on its entitlement to participate in dividends or return of capital.

s.561

s.560

This provision safeguards members, as their holdings of shares can only be diluted if they do not take up shares.

However, private companies may forgo these provisions in their articles of association and either substitute 'tailor-made' pre-emption provisions or delete pre-emption provisions entirely or may exclude the provisions by special resolution.

s.567

s.569

Public companies may only relax these provisions by special resolution. Many private companies are incorporated with articles of association that remove the statutory pre-emption rights and substitute alternative provisions. Commonly the first allotment following incorporation is exempt from any pre-emption provisions.

Where directors have been given authority to issue shares under s.551 either generally or by special resolution, they may be given power either in the articles or by special resolution to allot shares as if s.561 did not apply.

ss.570, 571

Listed companies and those whose shares are traded on AIM or PLUS will usually seek an annual renewal of a limited waiver of pre-emption rights to enable *ad hoc* share issues during the year.

These pre-emption provisions also apply to the sale of any treasury shares held by the company.

s.573

Checklist

- Do the articles exclude or vary the statutory pre-emption provisions of s.567? (Private companies only.)
- Is any previous waiver still valid, or has that authority been used by previous share issues or time expired?

- If the company has only a small number of shareholders it may be more practical to arrange for the shareholders to waive their pre-emption rights by notice in writing or written resolution as otherwise a general meeting will be required.
- If there is a shareholders' investment or similar agreement, this may contain pre-emption provisions that override the articles of association.

Procedure

- Convene a directors' meeting to recommend appropriate special resolution to waive pre-emption provisions to members and to seek members' approval by written resolution (private companies only) or at a general meeting. Ensure valid quorum present.
- Issue notice, signed by director or company secretary, on 14 clear days' notice (21 days if to be put to a public company's AGM) for members to consider resolution.   s.307
- Enclose with the notice a form of proxy if desired. Listed companies must enclose a three-way form of proxy (see page 176).
- If the meeting is to be convened on short notice, the company secretary should arrange for agreement to short notice to be signed by each of the shareholders.
- Hold general meeting. Ensure valid quorum is present. Resolution put to vote either by show of hands or by poll and to be passed by appropriate majority (special resolution by 75 per cent majority).
- Where circulated as a written resolution the requisite majority must be achieved with 28 days of circulation.   s.297
- Amend articles of association if necessary.

Filing requirement

- Copy of resolution within 15 days.   s.29
- Amended copy of articles of association if appropriate.   s.26

Notes

- It is not necessary to waive pre-emption rights for a rights, bonus or capitalisation issue as these are *pro rata* issues, except where overseas shareholders are excluded. For example many rights issues of publicly traded companies exclude overseas territories where to participate in the offer would require an offer document prepared under local laws to be registered in that overseas territory.

■ Where there is more than one class of shares, each class may have different pre-emption rights.

More information

Handbook: Chapter 5. Manual: Chapter 2.

Pre-emption rights – transfer

There are no statutory pre-emption rights on the transfer of shares. However, many private companies and some public companies will have pre-emption rights embodied within their articles of association. Although the provisions usually stipulate a strict procedure to follow when shares are to be transferred, these provisions are frequently waived in circumstances where the transfer is agreed by all the shareholders. The provisions would, however, be used in a contentious transfer. In such circumstances the pre-emption provisions must be followed strictly.

Checklist

- Check the articles of association to see whether pre-emption rights apply to the transfer.
- If the share transfer is not contentious, it may be appropriate for the existing shareholders to waive their rights of pre-emption by notice in writing.
- Alternatively, the transfer may be non-contentious, but due to the large number of shareholders the rights of pre-emption may best be waived by special resolution at a general meeting.

Procedure

- Where the transfer is likely to be contentious or it is deemed inappropriate or impractical to request that members waive their rights of pre-emption, it will be necessary to follow strictly the pre-emption procedure, as set down in the articles. These procedures will often take a number of weeks to complete and may require the company's auditors or accountant to certify a fair value for the shares.

Filing requirement

- None.

Notes

- Where a company's articles of association do contain

pre-emption rights on transfer, there may be special dispensations for transfers between family members or group companies.

■ Where shares are to be transferred following the death of a shareholder, the pre-emption provisions may be deemed to have been brought into effect and the shares offered to the existing shareholders even if the appropriate notice has not been given by the executor(s).

More information

Handbook: Chapter 5. Manual: Chapter 2.

Private or public company

The majority of companies are private companies limited by shares. However there are three types of private company, each with qualities better suited to certain activities than others. Additionally, rather than incorporating a company, entrepreneurs may prefer an unincorporated trading entity, such as a partnership or sole trader, or a mix of the two in the form of an LLP.

The following table shows the more common factors to consider when assessing what form of trading entity to use.

	Plc	Ltd	Un-limited	Guarantee	LLP	Unin-corporated
Is the company to trade for profit?	✓	✓	✓		✓	✓
Is it to be a charitable or non-profit-making body such as an association?				✓		✓
Is the liability of the members to be limited	✓	✓		✓	✓	
or unlimited? (Some professional associations require their members to trade without limited liability.)			✓			✓
Is financial information regarding the company to be kept confidential?: Yes			✓			✓
No	✓	✓		✓	✓	
Are the profits of the business to be assessed for tax on the owners?					✓	✓
Or the trading vehicle?	✓	✓	✓	✓		
Are shares in the business to be offered for subscription to the public (>50 persons)?	✓					
Or a defined, restricted membership?		✓	✓	✓	✓	✓

More information

Handbook: Chapter 1. Manual: Chapter 1.

Proxies

Members unable to attend a meeting can appoint one or more proxies to attend and vote in their place. A proxy need not be a member of the company.

s.324

A proxy can vote on a poll or on a show of hands. Proxies at private company meetings are usually entitled to speak at the meeting; however, proxies at public company meetings are not entitled to speak, other than to demand a poll.

ss.282(3)(b),
283(4)(b),
284(2)(b)

Companies need not appoint a proxy, as they may appoint a representative who may attend on their behalf with the same rights as if they were a shareholder in their own right. However, where a corporation wishes to appoint multiple appointees, making such appointments as proxies gives greater flexibility; as multiple corporate representatives, only one of them can exercise the voting rights.

s.323(1)

s.323(3)

Proxies can either be appointed with specific instructions on how to vote, or left to use their discretion.

The notice convening a members' meeting must disclose the members' rights to appoint proxies under s.324 or any more extensive rights contained in the company's articles of association.

s.325

Checklist

- Where a company issues proxy forms, they must be sent to all members entitled to vote at the meeting.

s.326

- Normally, proxies must be registered with the company not less than 48 hours prior to the meeting, and it is unlawful for the company to require that these be lodged more than 48 hours prior to the meeting excluding any day that is not a business day.

s.327(2)

Filing requirement

- None.

Notes

- Public companies listed on the Stock Exchange or AIM must
  issue three-way proxies.
- Most companies will word the proxy form to appoint the
  chairman as proxy, unless a specific person is chosen.
- Members can attend and vote in person even if they have lodged
  a proxy form, and attendance will often automatically revoke
  the appointment of a proxy. Accordingly a check should be made
  at the meeting to discard any proxies received from those
  attending.

LR 9.26, 13.28(a)

More information

📕 Handbook: Chapter 9. 📓 Manual: Chapters 1 and 14.

Purchase of own shares – out of capital

It is possible under certain circumstances for a private company to purchase its own shares out of capital, provided that the purchase is not restricted or prohibited by the company's articles of association. Additionally, there are restrictions on the company's ability to use its reserves to purchase its own shares and care must be taken to ensure that any profits available are utilised first as purchases out of capital can only be made (whether in whole or in part) if there are no distributable reserves available

ss.690, 709
s.710

Checklist

- Is the company a private company?
- Has the company no distributable reserves, or will the purchase use up all available distributable reserves?
- Check articles to ensure company is not prohibited from purchasing its own shares.
- Accounts must drawn up to a date within three months of the date of the directors' statement made under s.714 must be used to calculate the permissible capital payment.
- If the company's accounts are not audited, an auditors must be appointed.
- Will the directors be able to confirm the company's ability to pay its debts immediately after the payment and for the following 12 months, and will the auditors be able to confirm that such a statement is reasonable?

s.709(1)
s.710(1)

ss.712(6)
and (7)

ss.714(3)
and (6)

Procedure

- Convene a directors' meeting to approve the making of a statement specifying the permissible capital payment and confirming the company's ability to meet its debts, recommending the purchase to members and to either convene a general meeting or circulate a written resolution to obtain members approval. Ensure valid quorum present.

s.714

- Issue notice, signed by director or company secretary, on 14 clear days' notice, or circulate written resolution for members to consider special resolution(s). Included with the notice or written resolution must be an auditors' report and the terms of the purchase. The special resolution must be approved within one week of the date of the directors' statement made under s.714.   ss.716, 718

- Enclose with the notice a form of proxy if desired. Listed companies must enclose a three-way form of proxy (see page 176).

- A copy of the agreement, or a written schedule of its terms if the contract is not in writing, must be made available for inspection by the members of the company at the company's registered office for not less than 15 days prior to the meeting and at the meeting itself. The schedule of the terms must include the names of any members holding shares which it is proposed be purchased and, if the written contract does not show these names, a schedule must be attached showing the names and the number of shares to which the contract relates. Where a previously approved contract is being varied, the terms of the variation must be available for inspection by the members.   ss.693, 696(2)

- This requirement for the documents to be made available for inspection to the members prior to the meeting restricts the ability of the company to hold the meeting at shorter notice than 15 days. Where the resolutions are to be passed by written resolution of the members, a copy of the contract and/or any schedule must be supplied to the members no later than the date upon which they receive a copy of the written resolution for signature.   s.696(2)(b)

- Directors to make the statutory declaration specifying the permissible capital payment within one week before the date of the meeting.   s.714

- Hold general meeting. Ensure valid quorum is present. Resolution put to vote either by show of hands or by poll and to be passed by appropriate majority (special resolution by 75 per cent majority)   s.716

- Within one week of the passing of the special resolution the company must publish a notice in the *London Gazette* giving details of the proposed payment, and either notify creditors individually or by newspaper advertisement published within one week of the passing of the resolution. Creditors may make application to the court to cancel the resolution provided such application is made within five weeks of the date of approval of the special resolution.   s.719   s.721

- If an application is made, the court will decide whether to cancel   s.721(4) the resolution, reject the application or make such modification to the proposed purchase it deems appropriate.

- If no objections are received the payment may be made at the end of the five-week period and must be made within seven weeks of the date of approval of the special resolution. s.723(1)

- Once the company has purchased the shares, a return on form SH03 must be submitted to the Registrar, stating the number of shares and the class of shares together with the nominal value of the shares and the date on which they were re-purchased. The purchase of shares by a company is subject to stamp duty where the amount payable exceeds £1,000, the duty being payable on the consideration and not the nominal value at the rate of 0.5 per cent (rounded up to the nearest £5). s.707

- Issue consideration cheques and cancel share certificates relating to shares purchased. Update register of members.

Filing requirement

- Copy of special resolution within 15 days. s.30
- Amended copy articles of association, if amended. s.26
- Directors' and auditors' statement. s.714
- Notification in *London Gazette* of proposed payment. s.719(1)
- Advertisement in appropriate newspapers or notice given to all creditors. s.719(2)
- Stamped form SH03 within 28 days. s.707

Notes

- The resolution will be invalid if any member of the company holding shares which it is proposed be re-purchased exercises the voting rights attaching to those shares, and the resolution would not have been passed if those shares had not been voted. s.695
- Copies of the contracts must be retained for 10 years. s.702(3)

More information

Handbook: Chapter 5. Manual: Chapter 8.

See also reduction of capital on pages 185–188.

Purchase of own shares – out of profit

It is possible under certain circumstances for public and private companies to purchase their own fully paid shares, provided that the purchase is not restricted or prohibited by the company's articles of association. Additionally, there are restrictions on the company's ability to use its reserves to purchase its own shares and care must be taken to ensure that the company has sufficient distributable reserves for the purpose. It may also be possible for the company to issue new shares to fund the redemption. ss.690, 691 s.692(2)

Shares may be purchased as an off-market purchase in pursuance of a purchase contract approved in advance by members or by a market purchase on a recognised investment exchange s.693(1)

Checklist

- Has the company sufficient distributable reserves to fund the purchase?
- Check articles to ensure company is permitted to purchase its own shares.

Procedure – off-market purchase

- Convene a directors' meeting to recommend the purchase to members and to convene a general meeting or circulate a written resolution in the case of a private company. Ensure valid quorum present.
- Issue notice, signed by director or company secretary, on 14 clear days' notice for members to consider resolution(s). Where approval is being sought by written resolution, a copy of the purchase contract or the terms of the purchase must be circulated with the written resolution. ss.694, 696(2)(a)
- Enclose with the notice a form of proxy if desired. Listed companies must enclose a three-way form of proxy (see page 176).
- A copy of the agreement, or a written schedule of its terms if the contract is not in writing, must be made available for inspection s.696(2)(b)

by the members of the company at the company's registered office for not less than 15 days prior to the meeting and at the meeting itself. The schedule of the terms must include the names of any members holding shares which it is proposed be purchased and, if the written contract does not show these names, a schedule must be attached showing the names and the number of shares to which the contract relates. Where a previously approved contract is being varied, the terms of the variation must be available for inspection by the members.

- This requirement for the documents to be made available for inspection to the members prior to the meeting restricts the ability of the company to hold the meeting at shorter notice than 15 days.
- Hold general meeting. Ensure valid quorum is present. Resolution put to vote either by show of hands or by poll and to be passed by appropriate majority (special resolution by 75 per cent majority).
- Once the company has purchased the shares, a return on form SH03 must be submitted to the Registrar, stating the number of shares and the class of shares together with the nominal value of the shares and the date on which they were re-purchased. The re-purchase of shares by a company is subject to stamp duty, the duty being payable on the consideration and not the nominal value at the rate of 0.5 per cent (rounded up to the nearest £5).
- Issue consideration cheques and cancel share certificates relating to shares purchased. Update register of members.

Procedure – market purchase

- A company may only make a market purchase of its own shares if the purchase has been approved in advance by ordinary resolution.   s.701(1)
- The resolution may be a general authorisation or limited to the purchase of shares of a particular class or description and may also by an unconditional authority or conditional.   s.701(2)
- The authority must specify the maximum number of shares that may be purchased, the maximum and minimum process that may be paid and must specify the date not more than 18 months from the date of the resolution when the authority lapses.   ss.701(3), (5)

Filing requirement

- Copy of special resolution within 15 days.   s.30
- Amended copy articles of association, if amended.   s.26
- Stamped form SH03 within 28 days.   s.707

Notes

- In the case of a public company the resolution must state the date upon which the authority is to lapse, being not more than 18 months from the date of the resolution.   s.694(5)
- The resolution will be invalid if any member of the company holding shares which it is proposed be repurchased exercises the voting rights attaching to those shares, and the resolution would not have been passed if those shares had not been voted.   s.695
- Where a contract for an off-market purchase of shares has been approved a copy of the contract or, if not in writing, a written memorandum of its terms must be kept at the registered office or another specified place for at least ten years commencing on the date the purchase of shares was completed or the contract otherwise determines.   s.702

More information

Handbook: Chapter 5. Manual: Chapter 8.

Quorum – directors' meetings

The quorum for a meeting is the minimum number of directors that must be present and entitled to vote in order to constitute a valid meeting. The articles will normally stipulate the quorum. Unless modified, the default quorum established by the model articles for both private and public companies is two directors. Table A also provides for the directors to change the quorum as they see fit however any resolution to raise or lower the quorum must be taken at which a quorum is present.

reg.11 Sch.1,
reg.10 Sch.3
SI 2008/3229

If the articles are silent on the question of a quorum and specifically preclude the provisions of the model articles then the quorum will default to a majority of the directors in office from time to time.

The quorum must be maintained during the course of a meeting, if the number of directors present falls below the quorum the meeting must stand adjourned until a quorum (not necessarily the same directors) is present. This can be difficult where directors are interested in the business before the meeting and excluded from voting and from being counted in the quorum.

Checklist

- Is a quorum present?
- Is a quorum maintained and present for each item of business especially in circumstances where one or more directors may have a conflict of interests?
- If a director is also an alternate for another director, they will not count as 'two' people, for the purposes of determining whether a quorum is present, unless there is specific power in the articles.
- Directors 'present' by telephone/video conferencing etc will be included in the quorum.

Filing requirement

- None.

More information

☐ Manual: Chapter 2. ☐ Handbook: Chapter 13.

Quorum – shareholders' meetings

The quorum for a meeting is the minimum number of members that must be present and entitled to vote, in order to constitute a valid meeting. In the absence of any provisions in the articles of association, the default quorum is two members, or where the company has only one member the quorum is reduced to one.

s.318

None of the model articles specify a quorum.

The model articles for both private and public companies waive the quorum requirement on any resolution to appoint a chairman for the meeting.

reg. 38 Sch.1, reg. 30 Sch.3 SI 2008/3229

The model articles require the quorum to be present within half an hour of the time at which the meeting was due to start, and if not, the chairman must adjourn the meeting. When adjourning a meeting the chairman must stipulate either the time and place to which it is adjourned, or state that the meeting will continue at a time and place fixed by the directors.

reg. 41 Sch.1, reg. 33 Sch.3 SI 2008/3229

Occasionally the articles will stipulate that at the adjourned meeting those members attending, if any, shall constitute a valid quorum.

Checklist

- Check articles to establish quorum.
- Is a quorum present at the time the meeting has been convened to be held?
- If not present, is a quorum present within half an hour?
- Is a quorum maintained throughout the meeting?

Filing requirement

- None.

More information

☐ Handbook: Chapter 9. ☒ Manual: Chapter 14.

Reduction of capital – without court approval

Private companies are able to reduce their share capital, in any way, without requiring confirmation by the court. The members must approve the reduction by special resolution supported by a solvency statement made by the directors. The solvency statement option provides a simpler, cheaper and quicker alternative for a private company to reduce its share capital compared to the alternative requiring court approval (see page 187).

s.641(1)(a)

The solvency statement which must be signed by all directors states that in the directors' opinion the company is able to meet its debts on the date of the statement and will continue to be able to pay its debts as they fall due for the period of 12 months from the date of the statement.

s.643

Directors making a solvency statement, delivered to Companies House, without having reasonable grounds for the opinions stated, commit an offence.

Checklist

- Following the reduction, the company must still have some shares in issue.
- Are all the directors able to give the solvency statement?
- If appropriate, can the parent company provide additional comfort by way of a letter of support?
- Do the articles place any restriction on a reduction of capital?

s.641(2)

Procedure

- Convene a directors' meeting to recommend appropriate resolution(s) to members, to approve the solvency statement and to convene a general meeting. Ensure valid quorum present.
- Issue notice, signed by director or company secretary, together convening the general meeting on 14 clear days' notice for members to consider resolution. Alternatively, circulate the resolutions by written resolution.

ss.281, 307

- Enclose with the notice a form of proxy if desired (see page 175).
- Consider whether class meeting(s) also required.
- If the meeting is to be convened on short notice, the company secretary should arrange for agreement to short notice to be signed by the appropriate number of the shareholders (see page 153)   s.307(5)
- Where a general meeting is being held, ensure a valid quorum is present. Resolution put to vote either by show of hands or by poll and to be passed by appropriate majority (special resolution by 75 per cent majority).
- Copy of the special resolution, solvency statement, memorandum of capital and an additional directors' statement to be forwarded to Companies House. The reduction does not take effect until the resolutions are registered by Companies House.   s.644(1), (5)   s.644(4)

Filing requirements

- Special resolution.
- Solvency statement.
- Memorandum of capital.
- Directors' statement.

More information

Handbook: Chapter 4. Manual: Chapter 2.

Reduction of capital – with court approval

Public companies and private companies may reduce their share capital, in any way, by special resolution of their members subject to court approval. Private companies where the directors can give a solvency statement can take advantage of a simplified process (see page 185).

s.641(1)(b)

As part of the court process the company secretary will be required to confirm that the necessary administrative procedures relating to the convening of any general meeting or circulation of written resolution(s) have been complied with.

If the reduction includes either the diminution of any liability on unpaid share capital or a payment to shareholders, creditors have the right to object unless the court directs otherwise.

s.645

Checklist

- Following the reduction, the company must still have some shares in issue.
- Do the articles place any restriction on a reduction of capital?

s.641(2)

Procedure

- Convene a directors' meeting to recommend appropriate form of resolution(s) to members, approve the solvency statement and to convene a general meeting. Ensure valid quorum present.
- Issue notice, signed by director or company secretary, together convening the general meeting on 14 clear days' notice for members to consider resolution. Alternatively circulate the resolutions by written resolution.
- Enclose with the notice a form of proxy if desired (see page 175).
- Consider whether class meeting(s) also required.
- If the meeting is to be convened on short notice, the company secretary should arrange for agreement to short notice to be signed by the appropriate number of the shareholders (see page 153).

ss. 281, 307

s.307(5)

- Where a general meeting is being held, ensure valid quorum is present. Resolution put to vote either by show of hands or by poll and to be passed by appropriate majority (special resolution by 75 per cent majority).
- Application is made to court to confirm the reduction. In reaching any direction the court will be concerned to ensure that creditors are protected. List of creditors must be prepared and filed with the court.
- Provided the court confirms the reduction, copies of the court order, special resolution and statement of capital must be forwarded to Companies House. The reduction does not take effect until the resolutions are delivered to Companies House or if ordered by the court on registration by the Registrar.   s. 649(3)
- The Registrar must certify the registration of the order and statement of capital .   s.649(5)

Filing requirements

- Court order.
- Special resolution.
- Solvency statement.
- Memorandum of capital.
- Directors' statement.

More information

Handbook: Chapter 4.   Manual: Chapter 2.

Register of members – rectification

The Act does not contain specific authority for a company to rectify the register of members. The courts may order rectification of the register of members by the removal or addition of a person from or to the register. Original orders will bear the seal of the court or, alternatively, a duly authenticated office copy of the order may be registered.

s.125

In practice, however, minor clerical errors are informally corrected on the register under the authority of a responsible officer following receipt by the company or its registrar of a duly completed from of request for rectification of transferee details following the registration of a transfer of shares.

Where there is a substantial difference between the registered details and the rectification request (i.e. completely different name and address) great care must be taken and unless there has been a patent error a court order should be obtained.

Checklist

- The order should be checked to ensure that the holding referred to corresponds with a registered shareholding in the company. Identification will be facilitated by returning the relevant share certificate.

Procedure

- The amendments authorised in the order should be made to the register of members and the date of the order and its registration should be entered as the authority for the amendment.
- The existing share certificate may be endorsed as appropriate although it is preferable that a new share certificate be prepared.
- The company's registration stamp should be affixed to the order, which should be returned to the sender together with the endorsed or replacement share certificate.

- If a dividend mandate is currently in force, it may be appropriate for this to be amended, cancelled or renewed.

Filing requirement

- None.

More information

Handbook: Chapter 12. Manual: Chapter 6.

Registered office

All companies must have an address at which legal documents can be served. This is known as the registered office. On incorporation, the first registered office will be the address detailed on form IN01. Any change in registered office must be notified to Companies House on form AD01, to be effective. The registered office must be situated in the country of registration.

s.86

s.87

The registered office address must be shown on the company's business stationery, emails and its website(s) (see page 112).

s.82
regs 6, 7
SI 2008/495

Checklist

- Is the proposed registered office address in the country of incorporation?

s.9(2)(b)

- Is the proposed address a physical building? PO box addresses are not permitted.
- Headed stationery must show the [new] registered office address within 14 days of any change.

s.87(2)

- The company's name must be displayed at the registered office.

reg.3
SI 2008/495

- Are the statutory registers kept at the registered office, if the registered office is changed, have the statutory registers been moved to the new location?
- If the registers are not/no longer kept at the registered office, notify Companies House (forms AD02, AD03).

Procedure

- Convene a directors' meeting to approve change in registered office address. Ensure valid quorum present.
- File form AD01.

Filing requirement

- Form AD01 within 14 days.

s.87

Notes

- Notify bankers, auditors, solicitors, HM Revenue & Customs (corporation tax, PAYE, share schemes, VAT) and other interested persons.
- The change does not become effective until the form is received and accepted as valid by the Registrar of Companies.   s.87(2)
- Documents delivered to the old address within fourteen days of the date of change are validly served on the company.   s.87(3)
- The company's headed stationery must show the new registered office address not later than 14 days after the date that the notice was submitted to the Registrar of Companies.   s.87(3)

More information

☐ Handbook: Chapter 1. ▤ Manual: Chapter 1.

Registration of charges (England and Wales)

Particulars of every charge to which Companies Act 2006 applies, created by a company registered in England and Wales, should, within 21 days of its creation, be delivered for registration to Companies House, together with any instrument creating or evidencing the charge. Similar provisions apply to charges created by companies registered in Scotland and Northern Ireland (see page 196).

It is the duty of the company that creates a charge, or acquires property that is subject to a charge, to deliver to the Registrar the prescribed particulars of the charge within 21 days of the charge's creation, or the acquisition, as the case may be. A filing fee (currently £13) is payable. Although the obligation of registration is placed on the company, any interested party may effect this and it is, in practice, usual for the chargee, debenture holder or trustees to deal with the registration to ensure that their position is fully protected. Where the property is situated and the charge is created outside the United Kingdom, the 21-day period runs from the date on which the copy of the instrument could, in due course of post and diligently despatched, have been received in the United Kingdom.

On receipt, the Registrar of Companies will enter details of the charge in the register kept for each company for the purpose and will also issue a certificate of registration, which states the amount thereby secured and is conclusive evidence that the registration requirements have been complied with. A copy of the certificate of registration must be endorsed by the company on every debenture or certificate of debenture stock secured by the registered charge.

s.860
s.870(1),(2)
s.860(1)

s.860(1)
s.870(1),(2)
s.860(2)
s.870(1)(b), (2)(b)

s.869(1), (5)

s.865

Checklist

- Charge must be registered within 21 days of creation by the company or the person to whose favour the charge is given.
- Check articles of association to ensure the company's capacity to create a charge on its assets is not restricted in any way. Many

Listed companies will have the borrowing powers restricted to a multiple of their balance sheet value.

Procedure

- Convene a directors' meeting to approve the creation of a charge over some or all of the company's assets. Ensure valid quorum present.
- The original security document must be delivered to Companies House for registration within 21 days of the date of creation of the security. The security document must be accompanied by 'the prescribed particulars of the charge', set out on form MG01 for most forms of charge, form MG08 for a series of debentures, form MG06 where property is acquired subject to an existing mortgage or charge, and form MG09 for a charge comprising property situated in Scotland or Northern Ireland where registration is also required in the country of situation of the property.   s.870
- If the security relates to real property, the security document or particulars of the security should also be sent to the Land Registry, or the appropriate charge registered at the Land Charges Registry.
- A copy of every instrument creating a charge requiring registration must be kept at the registered office or a specified place of inspection.   ss.875, 877(2)
- Details of the security must be entered in the register of charges (and register of debentures as appropriate), which must be made available for inspection free of charge by any creditor or shareholder of the borrower or upon payment of a fee of £3.50 per hour or part thereof by any other person or company.   s.876, 877(4)   s.877(4)   SI 2008/3007

Filing requirement

- Original security document within 21 days.
- Form MG01, MG06, MG08 or MG09 as appropriate, within 21 days.
- Filing fee £13.

Notes

- If a charge is not properly registered with the Registrar of Companies, any security on the company's property or undertaking conferred by the charge is void against the liquidator or administrator and any creditor of the company, but not the company itself.   s.874

- The court has power under the Companies Act 2006, on the application of a company or any interested person, to extend the time for registration of the charge or to rectify an omission or misstatement of any particular relating to a charge. s.873

More information

Handbook: Chapter 1. Manual: Chapter 1.
Companies House: GBA8.

Registration of charges (Scotland)

(For this topic, references to the Registrar of Companies or Companies House are to the Registrar of Companies in Scotland and the Companies House in Edinburgh.) Particulars of every charge to which the Companies Act 2006 applies, created by a company registered in Scotland, should, within 21 days of its creation, be delivered for registration to Companies House together with any instrument creating or evidencing the charge.

s.878

It is the duty of the company that creates a charge, or acquires property that is subject to a charge, to deliver to the Registrar the prescribed particulars of the charge within 21 days of the charge's creation, or the acquisition, as the case may be. A filing fee (currently £13) is payable. Although the obligation of registration is placed on the company, any interested party may effect this and it is, in practice, usual for the chargee, debenture holder or trustees to deal with the registration to ensure that their position is fully protected. Where the property is situated and the charge is created outside the United Kingdom, the 21-day period runs from the date on which the copy of the instrument could, in due course of post and diligently despatched, have been received in the United Kingdom.

s.886(1), (2)

s.878(2)

ss.884, 886(1)
(b), (2)(b)

On receipt, the Registrar of Companies will enter details of the charge in the register kept for each company for the purpose and will also issue a certificate of registration, which states the amount thereby secured and is conclusive evidence that the registration requirements have been complied with.

s.885(1), (4)

Checklist

- Charge must be registered within 21 days of creation.
- Check articles of association to ensure the company's capacity to create a charge on its assets is not restricted in any way. Many listed companies will have the borrowing powers restricted to a multiple of their balance sheet value.

Procedure

- Convene a directors' meeting to approve the creation of a charge over some or all of the company's assets. Ensure valid quorum present.
- The original security document must be delivered to Companies   s.886 House for registration within 21 days of the date of creation of the security. The security document must be accompanied by 'the prescribed particulars of the charge', set out on form MG01s for most forms of charge, form MG08s for a series of debentures and form MG06s where property is acquired subject to an existing mortgage or charge.
- If the security relates to real property, the security document or particulars of the security should also be sent to the Land Registry or the appropriate charge registered at the Land Charges Registry.
- A copy of every instrument creating a charge requiring registra-   ss.890, 892(2) tion must be kept at the registered office or a specified place of inspection.
- Details of the security must be entered in the register of charges   s.891, 892 (4) (and register of debentures as appropriate), which must be made available for inspection free of charge by any creditor or share-   s.892(4) holder of the borrower or upon payment of a fee of £3.50 per hour or part thereof by any other person or company.

Filing requirement

- Original security document within 21 days.
- Form MG01s, MG06s or MG08s as appropriate within 21 days.
- Filing fee £13.

Notes

- If a charge is not properly registered with the Registrar of   s.889 Companies, any security on the company's property or under- taking conferred by the charge is void against the liquidator or administrator and any creditor of the company, but not the company itself.
- The court has power under the Companies Act 2006, on the   s.888 application of a company or any interested person, to extend the time for registration of the charge or to rectify an omission or misstatement of any particular relating to a charge.

More information

Handbook: Chapter 1. Manual: Chapter 1.
Companies House: GBA8(S).

Related party transactions

Where a director or a person 'connected' with a director acquires a non-cash asset from the company, or disposes of such an asset to the company, in most instances shareholder approval must be sought.

s.190(1)

Where the transaction has a value of more than £5,000 and exceeds the lower limit of £100,000, or 10 per cent of the company's net assets, shareholder approval is necessary.

s.191(2)

If the director or the connected person is also a director of the company's holding company, then approval of the members of the holding company must also be sought.

s.190(2)

Procedure

- Convene a directors' meeting to recommend appropriate special resolution to members and to convene a general meeting or seek approval by written resulution in the case of a private company. Ensure valid quorum present.
- Issue notice, signed by director or company secretary, on 14 clear days' notice for members to consider resolution.

s.307

- Enclose with the notice a form of proxy if desired.
- If the meeting is to be convened on short notice, the company secretary should arrange for agreement to short notice to be signed by each of the shareholders.

s.307(5)

- Hold general meeting. Ensure valid quorum is present. Resolution put to vote either by show of hands or by poll and to be passed by appropriate majority (ordinary resolution by 50 per cent majority).

S.282

Filing requirement

- None.

Notes

- Transactions between companies of a wholly owned group do not require approval.

s.192

- Where a transaction has not received approval of the members the transaction will usually be voidable by the company.   s.195

- Where a transaction was not approved in advance it may be affirmed by members within a reasonable period.   s.196

- Transactions undertaken on behalf of the director or connected person on a recognised stock exchange by an 'independent' broker do not require approval.

- Where a director acquires a non-cash asset by virtue of being a member of the company approval is not required.   s.192

- Any arrangements entered into which have not received prior or retrospective approval between a director, connected person or holding company and the company, make that director or connected person liable to the company for any gain arising out of the transaction or any losses suffered by the company.   s.195

More information

Handbook: Chapter 2. Manual: Chapters 11 and 16.

Re-registration – limited company as unlimited

Provided all members consent, a private limited company may be re-registered as an unlimited company.

s.102

In practice this is seldom done, however companies may chose to do so to keep their financial affairs secret (as unlimited companies do not need to file their accounts). Additionally, prior to dissolution, conversion to unlimited status can facilitate the return of funds to shareholders that otherwise might not be possible as a limited company due to the constraints on distribution of profit and return of capital.

Checklist

- If the company has previously re-registered from unlimited to limited this cannot be reversed.

s.102(2)

- Will all members consent to the change?

s.102(1)(a)

- Change company's stationery to reflect new status (see page 112).

Procedure

- Convene a directors' meeting to recommend appropriate resolutions to members and to convene a general meeting or circulate a written resolution. Additionally, resolutions to make certain amendments to the articles will be required to reflect the company's new status. Ensure valid quorum present.

s.302

- Where a general meeting is to be held, issue notice, signed by director or company secretary, on 14 clear days' notice for members to consider resolutions.

s.307(1)

- Enclose with the notice a form of proxy if desired.
- If the meeting is to be convened on short notice, the company secretary should arrange for agreement to short notice to be signed by each of the member.

s.307(5)

- Hold general meeting. Ensure valid quorum is present. Resolution put to vote either by show of hands or by poll and to be passed by unanimous consent of all members.

s.102(1)(a)

- Application is then made to the Registrar of Companies on form RR05 within 15 days, together with a copy of the resolution detailing the alterations to the articles of association appropriate for an unlimited company and an amended copy of the articles, together with a fee (currently £20).   ss.26, 103,

- Each member of the company must confirm in writing on the form RR05 that they wish the company to be re-registered as an unlimited company, together with a statement of compliance by the directors that every member has agreed to the re-registration, either personally or by their duly authorised agent   s.103(4)

- If accepted, the Registrar issues a new certificate of incorporation stating the company's unlimited status, whereupon the alterations to the articles of association set out in the application take effect. There is no need for the members to pass a special resolution approving these amendments.   s.104

Filing requirement

- Form RR05.
- Filing fee £20.
- Copy resolution.   s.103
- Amended copy of memorandum and articles of association.   s.26

Notes

- Unlimited companies do not normally need to file a copy of their accounts with the Registrar of Companies.
- Once the Registrar has issued the certificate of re-registration, it will be necessary to obtain new headed stationery, and a new company seal where the company has a seal.
- Arrange for the name of the company's bank accounts to be changed.
- Notify the company's suppliers and customers of the change of name, HM Revenue & Customs for corporation tax, PAYE and VAT, pension scheme, title deeds, trade mark registrations, data protection registration, insurers, etc. Signs at the company's premises or on the company's cars, vans and lorries will also require amendment.

More information

Handbook: Chapter 1. Manual: Chapter 1.

Re-registration – private company as public

Provided that a private limited company can satisfy five conditions, it can, by special resolution of the members, re-register as a public limited company.

ss.90, 97

Recently issued shares issued for a non-cash consideration may need to have the consideration valued.

s.93

Checklist

- Does the company have share capital?

s.90(2)(a)

- The issued share capital of the company must have a nominal value of at least £50,000 or the prescribed euro equivalent, and each share must be paid up to at least 25 per cent of its nominal value, together with all of any premium.

ss.90(2)(b), 91, 763, reg.2 SI 2008/729

- The application for re-registration must be received by the registrar of companies within seven months of its year-end and a copy of an audited balance sheet must be filed on or before the date of application for re-registration. Normally the balance sheet is taken from the latest audited accounts; however, a balance sheet may be submitted made up to an appropriate date not more than seven months prior to the application.

ss.90(2)(c), 92

- The company's auditors must give a statement to the effect that the net assets of the company are not less than its called-up share capital and undistributable reserves and, where the audit report to the audited accounts is qualified, that the subject of their qualification is not material for determining that the assets are greater than the called-up share capital and undistributable reserves.

s.92

- If shares have been issued otherwise than for cash during the period between the balance sheet date and the date of application for re-registration the provisions of s.593 must be complied with. These require an independent valuer to value the consideration received by the company. These provisions do not apply to a share exchange or proposed merger with another company.

s.90(2)(d)

s.593

s.93(2)(b)

- The company must not previously have been re-registered as an unlimited company. — s.90(2)(e)
- If it does not already have one, a company secretary must be appointed. — s.271

Procedure

- Convene a directors' meeting to recommend appropriate special resolution to members and to convene a general meeting or circulate a written resolution. Additionally, resolutions to make certain amendments to the articles will be required to reflect the company's new status. Ensure valid quorum present. — s.302
- Issue notice, signed by director or company secretary, on 21 clear days' notice for members to consider resolution. — s.307(1)
- Enclose with the notice a form of proxy, if desired.
- If the meeting is to be convened on short notice, the company secretary should arrange for agreement to short notice to be signed by each of the shareholders. — s.307(5)
- Hold general meeting. Ensure valid quorum is present. Resolution put to vote either by show of hands or by poll and to be passed by appropriate majority (special resolution by 75 per cent majority)
- File all necessary documents, as set out below, with Companies House within 15 days of passing the resolutions. — s.30
- If accepted, the Registrar issues a new certificate of incorporation stating the company's plc status, whereupon the alterations to the memorandum and articles of association set out in the application take effect. There is no need for the members to pass a special resolution approving these amendments. — s.96

Filing requirement

Form RR01.

- A copy of the relevant balance sheet.
- A copy of the audit report.
- A copy of the auditors' statement.
- A copy of the amended articles of association.
- A copy of special resolutions.
- Re-registration fee (currently £20; same-day fee £80).

Notes

- A company which has been re-registered as unlimited cannot subsequently re-register as a public company. — s.90(2)(e)

- If the company has insufficient share capital, additional shares must be issued. This is often achieved by a bonus issue (see page 46), as a company seeking re-registration will normally have adequate reserves. s.763
- There is no obligation for a public company's shares to be quoted. Many private companies re-register for the marketing advantages of being a Plc.
- The regulations governing Plcs, the actions of their directors and the preparation of accounts are more onerous than for private companies.
- Once the Registrar has issued the certificate of re-registration, it will be necessary to obtain new headed stationery, and a new company seal where the company has a seal.
- Arrange for the name of the company's bank accounts to be changed.
- Notify the company's suppliers and customers of the change of name HM Revenue & Customs for corporation tax, PAYE and VAT, pension scheme, title deeds, trade mark registrations, data protection registration, insurers, etc. Signs at the company's premises or on the company's cars, vans and lorries will also require amendment.

More information

☐ Handbook: Chapter 1. 📕 Manual: Chapter 1.

Re-registration – public company as private

This procedure is becoming more common, as more stringent and restrictive provisions for public companies, in particular accounting provisions, continue to increase their scope and effect.

There are no particular qualifying criteria, and all public companies, subject to any other regulatory requirements such as FSA, UKLA etc, could be re-registered as private companies.   s.97

A public company can register as a private company limited by shares or guarantee or as a private unlimited company.   s.89(b), (e)

Procedure

Change to private limited

- Convene a directors' meeting to recommend appropriate special   ss.97, 302
  resolution to members and to convene a general meeting.
  Additionally, resolutions to make certain amendments to the
  articles will be required to reflect the company's new status.
  Ensure valid quorum present.
- Issue notice, signed by director or company secretary, on 14 clear   s.307(1)
  days' notice for members to consider resolution. Twenty-one
  days' notice if the resolution(s) are to be put at an annual general
  meeting.
- Enclose with the notice a form of proxy if desired.
- If the meeting is to be convened on short notice, the company   s.307(5
  secretary should arrange for agreement to short notice to be
  signed by each of the shareholders.
- Hold general meeting. Ensure valid quorum is present. Resolution put to vote either by show of hands or by poll and to be
  passed by appropriate majority (special resolution by 75 per cent
  majority)
- File all necessary documents with Companies House within 15   s.30
  days of passing the resolution.
- Within 28 days of the passing of the resolution an application
  may be made to the court for the cancellation of the resolution.

This application may be made only by a holder or holders of at least 5 per cent of the issued share capital of the company (or of any class of shares) or by not less than 50 of the company's members. If such an application is made, the court may confirm or cancel the resolution or impose certain conditions on its approval. The company must file a copy of any order made by the court with the Registrar within 15 days of the making of the order or within such period as may be determined by the court. `s.98`

- If no application is made to the court within 28 days of the passing of the resolution, an application for re-registration as a private company should be submitted to the Registrar on form RR02, signed by a director or secretary, together with a copy of the amended articles of association. If all shareholders voted in favour of the resolution form RR02 may be filed immediately. `s.97(1)(c), (2)`
- If accepted, the Registrar issues a new certificate of incorporation stating the company's limited status, whereupon the alterations to the memorandum and articles of association set out in the application take effect. There is no need for the members to pass a special resolution approving these amendments. `s.101`

Change to private unlimited

The procedure for a re-registration as a private unlimited company are the same as for re-registering as a private limited company except as follows:

- The resolution to re-register requires consent of all members entitled to vote; `s.109(1)(a)`
- The company must not previously have been re-registered as a private limited or unlimited company; and `s.109(2)` `s.110`
- The application form is form RR05.

Filing requirement

- A copy of special resolution.
- Form RR02 or RR05.
- A copy of amended articles of association.
- Statement of compliance.
- A copy of court order, if appropriate.
- Re-registration fee (currently £20; same-day fee £80).

Notes

- Once the Registrar has issued the certificate of re-registration, it will be necessary to obtain new headed stationery, and a new company seal where the company has a seal.

- Arrange for the name of the company's bank accounts to be changed.
- Notify the company's suppliers and customers of the change of name HM Revenue & Customs for corporation tax, PAYE and VAT, pension scheme, title deeds, trade mark registrations, data protection registration, insurers, etc. Signs at the company's premises or on the company's cars, vans and lorries will also require amendment.
- In addition to the voluntary re-registration as a private company, a public company may be required to re-register by the court where its issued share capital is below the authorised minimum. This would normally only occur on a reduction of capital or redemption of redeemable shares. In such an event the court may authorise the re-registration to be effective without a special resolution being passed and may specify in the order the amendments to be made to the memorandum and articles of association.

s.650

More information

Handbook: Chapter 1. Manual: Chapter 1.

Resolutions – filing requirements

A copy of the following resolutions must be filed with the Registrar of Companies within 15 days of approval.   s.30

Checklist

- Special resolutions.   s.29
- Resolutions or agreements which have been agreed to by all the members of a company, but which, if not so agreed to, would not have been effective for their purpose unless (as the case may be) they had been passed as special resolutions.
- Resolutions or agreements which have been agreed to by all the members of some class of shareholders but which, if not so agreed to, would not have been effective for their purpose unless they had been passed by some particular majority or otherwise in some particular manner, and all resolutions or agreements which effectively bind all the members of any class of shareholders though not agreed to by all those members.   s.67
- A resolution passed by the directors of a company in compliance with a direction to change name by Secretary of State.
- A resolution of a company to give, vary, revoke or renew an authority to the directors for allotment of relevant securities.   ss.550, 551
- A resolution conferring, varying, revoking or renewing authority for market purchase of company's own shares.   s.701
- A resolution for voluntary winding-up.   s.84 IA 1986

More information

Handbook: Chapter 9. Manual: Chapters 14.
Companies House: GBA7.

Resolutions – majority

The majorities required to pass resolutions are as follows.

Checklist

■ Ordinary resolutions: simple majority.   s.282
■ Special resolutions: 75 per cent majority.   s.283

Notes

■ The majority for type of resolution is of those members entitled to attend and vote *and* present and voting at a general meeting in person or by proxy.

■ At a meeting on a show of hands each member or their proxy has one vote.   ss.282(3), 283(4)

■ On a poll vote each member or their proxy has one vote per share.   ss.282(4), 283(5)

■ For written resolution of a private company, the majority is calculated by reference to each member's total voting rights.   ss.282(2), 283(2)

More information

📖 Handbook: Chapter 9. 📓 Manual: Chapters 14.

Resolutions – written: private companies

A private company may, by written resolution of members, pass resolutions which would otherwise require a general meeting to be held.

ss.282, 283, 288

Checklist

- Is the company a private company?
- Are sufficient members available to sign the written resolution?

Procedure

- Written resolutions must be approved by members representing sufficient voting rights to meet the simple or 75 per cent majority required for ordinary and special resolutions respectively.

ss.282(2), 283(2)

- The signatures need not all appear on the same document, provided that all the signed documents are in the same form, the resolution is effective and dated when signed by or on behalf of the last member to sign.
- If the appropriate majority has not been reached within twenty eight days of the date of circulation the resolution lapses.

s.297

- The original signed copies of a written resolution should be inserted in the company's minute book in the normal manner.
- As the majority of resolutions for a private company may now be passed by written resolution, certain changes have been necessitated to the circulation of documentation to shareholders. Accordingly, documents that are required to be circulated to shareholders with a notice of a general meeting or are to be made available at the company's registered office for inspection prior to the meeting must, where a written resolution is to be used, be circulated to each member before or at the same time as the resolution is supplied for signature. Such documents include the following:
  - ☐ a written statement to be given by directors pursuant to a special resolution, waiving the rights of pre-emption on the allotment of shares;

s.571(6)

- ☐ a copy of the purchase contract, or written memorandum of its terms relating to the off-market purchase or contingent purchase by a company of its own shares; s.701
- ☐ a declaration of compliance and auditors' report relating to the purchase by a company of its own shares out of capital; s.718
- ☐ solvency statement by directors in support of a non-court reduction of capital; s.641
- ☐ a written memorandum setting out the terms of a proposed director's service contract for a term of more than two years;
- ☐ disclosure of matters relating to the approval of a director's expenditure to enable them properly to perform their duties.

Filing requirement

- ■ Copy of resolution signed by all shareholders within 15 days. s.30

Notes

- ■ There are two resolutions that cannot be passed by a written resolution under any circumstances:
  - ☐ the removal of a director pursuant to s.168 before the expiration of his period of office;
  - ☐ the removal of an auditors under s.510 before the expiration of his period of office.
- ■ Where any particular member is interested in the matter to be approved by written resolution and would not be eligible to vote at a general meeting, they are similarly barred from voting by written resolution on the same matter.

More information

📕 Handbook: Chapter 9. 📖 Manual: Chapters 14.

Restoration – administrative

Where a company has been struck off the Register and dissolved using the procedures set out in s.1000 or s.1001, the former directors or former members may apply to the Registrar to have the company restored to the Register. Such application must be made within six years of the date of dissolution of the company.

s.1024(1),(2)

s.1024(4)

It should be noted that where a company has been wound up and dissolved, any application for restoration must made by to the court, see page 214.

s.1029

Prior to restoration it will be necessary to bring the company's statutory records up to date. This will normally involve the completion of all outstanding annual returns and the preparation of accounts as well as any changes in shareholdings, officers or other statutory details of the company to be filed and obtaining the consent of the Treasury solicitor if any property has vested *bona vacantia*.

s.1025

Checklist

- If dissolved under s.1000 or s.1001 restoration application must be within six years.

  s.1024(1)

- The company must have been carrying on business or in operation at the time of dissolution.

  s.1025(2)

- The Crown representative, usually the Treasury solicitor, must consent in writing to the restoration where any property has vested *bona vacantia*.

  s.1025(3)

- All documents required to bring the company's record at Companies House up to date must be delivered to the Registrar together with payment of any filing penalties outstanding at the date of dissolution.

  s.1025(5)

Procedure

- Ensure conditions of s.1025 have been met and all appropriate documents lodged with the Registrar.

  s.1026 (1)

- File form RT01 together with a statement of compliance that the requirements for administrative restoration are met.

  s.1026(2)

- If the Registrar decides that the application is successful written

  s.1027

confirmation is issued to the applicant and the company's name is restored to the Register of companies together with publication of that fact in the *Gazette*.

Filing requirement

- All necessary forms, annual returns and accounts to bring the company's records up to date.
- Late filing penalties as appropriate.
- Restoration fee, currently £300.

Notes

- In addition to the restoration fee payable to the Registrar of Companies, the company will also be required to pay the costs of the Crown representative, if any and the penalties for late submission of accounts, as appropriate. Where late filing penalties are levied in respect of accounts required to be filed prior to restoration these are at the minimum statutory penalty rate.
- In practice restoration is often required where a company has been dissolved by the Registrar (for failure to file returns and/or accounts) or at the request of the directors/shareholders and it is subsequently found that the company has valuable assets. In these circumstances, it is necessary for the company to be restored to the Register for the assets to be reclaimed, as the assets of a dissolved company automatically attach to the Crown. It is becoming increasingly common for a company with assets to be dissolved as a result of oversight on the part of directors; either neglect in filing statutory documents, or requesting the director to strike off the company without properly checking that the company has no assets. For example, particular care should be taken when requesting the dissolution of a subsidiary that the legal ownership of property has passed to its holding company or fellow subsidiary. It is not uncommon for the appropriate book entries to be made, for example, transferring the lease of a property to another group company without ensuring that the legal transfer of title is also effected.

More information

Handbook: Chapter 1. Manual: Chapter 19.
Companies House: GBW2.

Restoration – by court order

Application to the court may be made to restore a company:

- dissolved under the Insolvency Acts;   s.1029(1)
- dissolved at the conclusion of an administration; or
- dissolved either by the registrar under ss.1000 or 1001 or under   s.1024(4)
  the voluntary dissolution procedures under s.1003

Application is made to a the High Court, usually the Registrar of Companies Court in London. Cases can also be heard in district registries or county courts that have authority to wind up a company.

Application may be made by any person having an interest in the   s.1029(2)
company, including the Secretary of State, former directors or members, any creditor, former liquidator, persons with contractual arrangements with the company, managers or trustees of pension funds etc.

Prior to restoration it will be necessary to bring the company's statutory records up to date. This will normally involve the completion of all outstanding annual returns and the preparation of audited accounts as well as any changes in shareholdings, officers or other statutory details of the company to be filed.

Checklist

- Restoration to pursue personal injury claims may be made at any   s.1030(1)
  time.
- Except as noted below, in all other cases application must be   s.10304
  made within six years of the date of dissolution of the company.
- The exception is where a company was dissolved under ss.1000   s.1030(5)
  or 1001 and an application for administrative restoration under s.1024 has been rejected. In such circumstances an application to court must be made within 28 days of the notice of the decision by the Registrar to reject the application under s.1024

Procedure

- The restoration process requires an application to the court and accordingly the services of a solicitor are required. In the circumstances the procedure is not detailed here.

Filing requirement

- All necessary forms, annual returns and accounts to bring the company's records up to date.
- Late filing penalties as appropriate.

Notes

- In addition to the restoration fee payable to the Registrar of Companies (currently £300), the company will also be required to pay the legal costs of the Registrar (currently between £250 and £300) and the penalties for late submission of accounts, as appropriate. Where late filing penalties are levied in respect of accounts required to be filed prior to restoration, these are at the minimum statutory penalty rate.
- In practice, restoration is often required where a company has been dissolved by the Registrar (for failure to file returns and/or accounts) or at the request of the directors/shareholders and it is subsequently found that the company has valuable assets. In these circumstances, it is necessary for the company to be restored to the Register for the assets to be reclaimed, as the assets of a dissolved company automatically attach to the Crown. It is becoming increasingly common for a company with assets to be dissolved as a result of oversight on the part of directors; either neglect in filing statutory documents, or requesting the director to strike off the company without properly checking that the company has no assets. For example, particular care should be taken when requesting the dissolution of a subsidiary that the legal ownership of property has passed to its holding company or fellow subsidiary. It is not uncommon for the appropriate book entries to be made, for example, transferring the lease of a property to another group company without ensuring that the legal transfer of title is also effected.
- Occasionally, a company that has been dissolved will be found to have a large outstanding creditor. In such circumstances the creditor may apply to the court to have the company restored to the Register at the company's cost, to enable him to pursue the claim.

More information

📖 Handbook: Chapter 1. 📘 Manual: Chapter 19.
Ⓒ Companies House: GBW2.

Rights issue

A rights issue is an issue of shares to the existing shareholders pro rata to their existing holdings.

Rights issues are used by companies to obtain additional funding from the company's shareholders, rather than obtaining working capital by borrowing from banks or other financial institutions.

Checklist

- Check the articles to ensure there is no restriction on the maximum number of shares that may be issued. If not it will be necessary to increase or remove that restriction (see page 143).
- Check the articles of association to ensure the directors have authority in terms of s.550 or s.551 to issue shares. If not a resolution to renew the authority will be required (see page 143).
- If the company has overseas shareholders it may be necessary to exclude them from the rights issue due to securities legislation in their country, in which case the company must have sufficient waiver of pre-emption rights in terms of ss.567 to 571.
- If the rights issue is to be made by way of renounceable letters of allotment, the articles of association must be checked to ensure that no pre-emption rights on allotment are infringed.

Procedure

- Convene a directors' meeting to approve resolutions declaring the rights issue and resolve to issue the provisional allotment letters to the company's shareholders. Ensure valid quorum present.
- If it is intended that the existing members may renounce their entitlement to third parties, these letters include letters of renunciation.
- Once the closing date for the acceptance of the allotment letters has been reached, the directors will meet to allot those shares taken up.
- The company secretary should ensure that appropriate share certificates are prepared and issued to the shareholders, and that

s.555

form SH01 is filed with the Registrar of Companies within 15 days.

■ The company secretary should ensure that the register of members is written up to reflect the issue of shares.

Filing requirement

■ Form SH01.
■ Copies of any ordinary and special resolutions, as necessary.   s.30

More information

📖 Handbook: Chapter 5. 📖 Manual: Chapter 3.

Sensitive words

Certain words and phrases ('sensitive' words) require the consent of the Secretary of State for Trade and Industry before their use is allowed in a company name. Alternatively, the Secretary of State may require that appropriate authority be obtained from a relevant body.

ss.54, 55

The sensitive words that require the consent of the Secretary of State for Trade and Industry are:

- words that imply national or international pre-eminence;
- words which imply governmental patronage or sponsorship;
- words which imply business pre-eminence or representative status;
- words which imply specific objects or functions.

For a company to use one or more of these words in its name, its use must be justified.

The Registrar of Companies has issued guidelines giving details of the criteria to be used and these are set out below. It should be noted, however, that these are not definitive criteria and in every case the decision on whether or not to allow a particular name to be used will rest with the Secretary of State for Trade and Industry.

Checklist

- Words which imply national or international pre-eminence:

British	Welsh
Great	English
Britain	Ireland
National	Scottish
Wales	European
England	Irish
International	United
Scotland	Kingdom

- Words which imply business pre-eminence or representative or authoritative status:

Association	Federation
Authority	Institute
Board	Institution
Council	Society

- Words which imply specific objects or functions:

Assurance	Insurer
Assurer	Patent
Benevolent	Patentee
Charter	Post office
Chartered	Reassurance
Chemist	Re-assurer
Chemistry	Register
Co-operative	Registered
Foundation	Re-insurance
Friendly society	Re-insurer
Fund	Sheffield
Group	Stock exchange
Holding	Trade union
Industrial and provident society	Trust
Insurance	

- Words or expressions in the following list need the approval of the Secretary of State.

Abortion	Nurse
Architect	Nursing
Building Society	Occupational Therapist
Chamber(s) of Business	Olympiad
Chamber(s) of Commerce	Olympiads
Chamber(s) of Commerce	Olympian
Chamber(s) of Commerce and Industry	Olympians
	Olympic
Chamber(s) of Enterprise	Olympics
Chamber(s) of Industry Chamber(s) of Trade	Ophthalmic Optician
	Optician
Chamber(s) of Trade and Industry	Optometrist
	Orthoptist
Chamber(s) of Training	Patent Agent
Chamber(s) of Training and Enterprise	Patent Office
	Pharmaceutical
Charitable	Pharmaceutist

Charity
Chiropodist
Contact Lens
Credit Union
Credit Union Act 1979
Dental
Dental Practitioner
Dental Surgeon
Dentist
Dentistry
Dietician
Dispensing Optician
District Nurse
Drug
Druggist
Duke
Enrolled Optician
Geneva Cross
Health Service
Health Visitor
His/Her Majesty
Institute of Laryngology
Institute of Orthopaedics
Institute of Otology
Institute of Urology
King
Medical Laboratory
Midwife
Midwifery

Pharmacist
Pharmacy
Physiotherapist
Police
Pregnancy
Prince
Princess
Professions (if preceded
   by Registered State
   or Registered)
Queen
Radiographer
Red Crescent
Red Cross
Red Lion and Sun Anzac
Registered Optician
Remedial Gymnast
Royal
Royale
Royalty
Special School
Technician
Termination
Training and Enterprise
University
Vet Solicitor
Veterinary
Veterinary Surgeon
Windsor

Procedure

- Where any word or phrase requires the consent of the Secretary of State or from a relevant body advice should be sought from Companies House as to the form of the authority required.

More information

Handbook: Chapter 1, Appendix 6. Manual: Chapter 1.
Companies House: GBF2, GBF3.

Share certificate – duplicate

Share certificates are evidence of title, and so care must be taken when issuing duplicate certificates.

Checklist

- Check that there is no differences between the identity of the registered shareholder and the person requesting the duplicate.

Procedure

In the event of a shareholder losing his or her share certificate, the following procedure should be followed:

- The shareholder should be sent a form of indemnity in respect of the issue of a duplicate certificate. This is to protect the company, should the original share certificate fall into the wrong hands and an attempt be made to transfer the shares fraudulently.
- The form of indemnity should be signed by the shareholder and, for most quoted public limited companies, it will be necessary for the indemnity to be guaranteed by a bank or insurance company
- On receipt by the company of a completed indemnity form a duplicate share certificate should be prepared and issued to the shareholder.
- If the original share certificate is found, it should be returned to the company and cancelled.

Filing requirement

- None.

More information

Handbook: Chapter 8. Manual: Chapter 5.

Shareholders – probate

A company should accept for registration any grant of probate for confirmation, or a properly validated copy, provided that it bears the court seal.

Checklist

- A careful check must be made to ensure that the details shown on the grant of probate correspond with the entry in the register of members. If there is any doubt as to whether the deceased is indeed a shareholder of the company, then the company should obtain a declaration of identity from the executors. This will usually be given by the solicitors acting for the estate, although the deceased's bankers can also give a declaration of identity.

s.774

Procedure

- Details of the probate should be recorded in the company's document register.
- The date of death and the date of registration of the probate together with the name(s) and address(es) of the executor(s) should be noted in the register of members and the register should be amended to show the word 'deceased' after the shareholder's name. The postal address for correspondence should be amended to that of the executor and should be addressed to the 'Executor of [shareholder's name] deceased'.
- The share certificates should be endorsed with fact and date of death, the date of registration of probate and the name(s) and address(es) of the executor(s). The endorsement should be validated with the company's security seal.
- The company's security seal should be impressed on the probate and the probate together with the amended share certificate should be returned to the person who lodged them. A new dividend mandate form may also be enclosed as any existing mandate will have been revoked on the death of the shareholder.

Filing requirement

- None.

Notes

- The company may request that the executor(s) transfer the shares to themselves as this simplifies further requests and the need to validate instructions no longer applies. This transfer may, however, invoke the pre-emption provisions contained in the articles of association.

More information

Handbook: Chapter 8. Manual: Chapter 6.

Shares – application and allotment

Checklist

Prior to any allotment of shares, the directors should ensure that they have sufficient authority to allot shares and that the statutory pre-emption provisions on the allotment of shares or if different any provisions contained in the company's articles of association are not infringed or, to the extent that they are, that the necessary waivers have been received from the members, either in writing or in general meeting (see page 169).
ss.550, 551

s.561

If the company's articles restrict the aggregate number of issued shares, it will be necessary to convene a general meeting or circulate a written resolution in the case of a private company to remove the restriction, increase the directors' authority to allot shares and to waive any pre-emption rights as necessary (see page 109).

Procedure

- A form of application should be made available for those persons wishing to subscribe for shares. Private companies must take care when drafting an application letter to make sure that it is not regarded as an invitation to the public to subscribe for shares. Only public companies can issue shares to the public.
s.112

ss.755, 756
- Those persons wishing to subscribe for the shares will complete the application form and return this to the company, together with a cheque in full or part payment for the shares, as appropriate.
- Once the application forms and remittances have been received, the remittance cheques should be banked as soon as possible.
s.554
- Convene a directors' meeting to approve the applications, the issue of shares, issue of share certificates and updating of the register of members. Ensure valid quorum present.
- As soon as possible, share certificates should be issued to the applicants, and in any event not more than two months from the date of allotment.
s.769

- Public companies whose shares are publicly traded may have their shares held in uncertificated form in CREST.
- Within one month of the date of allotment a return of allotments (form SH01) should be filed with the Registrar of Companies. s.555
- If the shares are all fully paid, it will not be necessary for the shares to have distinguishing numbers.

Filing requirement

- Form SH01 within one month.

Notes

- Under certain circumstances, fully paid and partly paid shares of the same class may be regarded as two different classes of shares.

More information

Handbook: Chapter 5. Manual: Chapter 5.

Shares – consolidation

Occasionally, it will be necessary to consolidate the share capital of the company into shares of a greater nominal value. For instance, a consolidation of 4,000 25p shares into £1.00 shares will result in the authorised share capital being 1,000 shares of £1.00 each.

s.618

Occasionally, a quoted public limited company will consolidate its shares into shares of a higher nominal value, where the shares have a very low market price. The consolidation of the shares will effectively increase the market price and make it easier to trade in the shares.

Alternatively, consolidation of shares will be used in capital reconstruction or capital reduction schemes. For instance, a company may decide to reduce its capital from £1.00 shares to 50p shares and then consolidate the shares into £1.00 shares, thus achieving a 50 per cent capital reduction whilst retaining a nominal value of £1.00 for the shares.

Procedure

- Convene a directors' meeting to recommend appropriate ordinary resolution to members and to convene a general meeting or circulate a written resolution in the case of a private company. Ensure valid quorum present. s.302
- Issue notice, signed by director or company secretary, on 14 clear days' notice, for members to consider resolution. s.307
- Enclose with the notice a form of proxy if desired.
- If the meeting is to be convened on short notice, the company secretary should arrange for agreement to short notice to be signed by each of the shareholders. s.307(5)
- Hold general meeting. Ensure valid quorum is present. Resolution put to vote either by show of hands or by poll and to be passed by appropriate majority (ordinary resolution by 50 per cent majority).
- File copy of resolution and form SH02 at Companies House. ss.30, 619
- The register of members will require amendment to show details of the new number of shares and nominal value of the shares

currently held and any distinguishing numbers will require reallocation.

- If there are any fractions of shares arising upon the consolidation, these should be sold for the benefit of the members concerned or, alternatively, occasionally new shares can be issued, credited as fully paid, to round their holding up to the nearest whole number.
- All existing share certificates should be recalled, either for amendment or cancellation, new share certificates being issued.

Filing requirement

- Form SH02 within one month.

More information

Handbook: Chapter 4. Manual: Chapter 2.

Shares – convertible

As the name implies, these are shares that can be converted from one class to another, either at some specific time in the future, on the occurrence of a specific event, or at the option of the company or the shareholder.

ss.549, 550, 551

Convertible shares will often be issued so that the company can attract additional funds, with the shares being issued with enhanced dividend rights. After a period of time, the shares would be converted to ordinary shares, thus reducing the dividends payable by the company.

The issue of convertible shares is similar to loans to the company, but with repayment of the loan at the end of its term being replaced by conversion to ordinary shares.

Checklist

The following points should be considered when convertible shares are being created:

- whether the shares could carry pre-emption rights on allotment or transfer;
- the amount, if any, of dividend and whether this should be preferential;
- whether the shares should carry voting rights;
- whether the shares should carry a preferential right to the return of capital on any winding up or distribution and whether the shares should participate in any surplus;
- the terms of conversion, including whether conversion should be at the option of the company, the shareholder or both, or at predetermined dates, and the basis of conversion to ordinary shares;
- creation of the shares will require alterations to the articles of association and must be authorised by the shareholders by ordinary and special resolutions at a general meeting or by written resolution in the case of a private company;
- once the shares have been created any further changes to the articles of association may require approval of the holders of the

convertible shares at a separate class meeting, whether or not they are voting shares;

Procedure

■ The procedure to be followed on conversion of the shares is the same as that to be followed on the conversion of convertible loan stock (see page 141).

Filing requirement

■ Form SH01 on issue of shares.

More information

☐ Handbook: Chapters 4 and 5. ▦ Manual: Chapter 9.

Shares – cumulative

The dividend payable on such shares is 'cumulative', that is, any dividend not paid on the shares in one year will be accumulated and paid in succeeding years.

As dividends can be paid only out of distributable profits available for the purpose, the dividend may not be paid in a particular year as the company has insufficient distributable profit. In these circumstances the unpaid dividend will accumulate until such time as the company has sufficient distributable profit to pay a dividend and any arrears to date.

It would be unusual for cumulative shares not to have a fixed dividend, as the directors would only declare a discretionary dividend in the circumstances where the company has profits available for distribution.

Checklist

The following points should be considered when cumulative shares are being created:

- whether the shares should carry pre-emption rights on allotment or transfer;
- whether the shares will have a preferential right to the return of capital and whether this should be limited to the amounts paid up or credited as paid up on the shares or whether they should participate in any surplus;
- whether the shares should be voting shares;
- the amount of the fixed dividend and any preferential payment terms, i.e. before or after any dividend to be declared on any other class of shares;
- the creation of the shares will require alterations to the articles of association of the company. If the shares are to be created after the incorporation of the company, the creation of the shares will require the consent of the shareholders by ordinary and special resolutions at a general meeting or by written resolution in the case of a private company;
- any subsequent alteration to the articles may also require

approval of the holders of any cumulative shares if the alteration alters their class rights. This approval will be required at a separate class meeting and is required even where the particular class of shares are non-voting;

■ whether or not the shares should be redeemable or convertible at some future date.

More information

Handbook: Chapter 7. Manual: Chapter 7.

Shares – redeemable

A limited company having a share capital may, if authorised by its articles of association, issue shares which are redeemable or which are liable to be redeemed at the option of the company or the shareholder. The articles of a public company must include specific authority for the issue of redeemable shares.

s.684

s.684(3)

Checklist

- At the time of issue of redeemable shares there must be in issue shares that are not redeemable. This is to ensure that the issued share capital of the company cannot all be redeemed, leaving the company with no shareholders.

  s.684(4)

- Redeemable shares can only be redeemed if they are fully paid.

  s.686(1)

- The terms of redemption may provide for payment in cash on a date later than redemption, failing which they must be paid for on redemption.

  s.686(2), (3)

- Public companies may only redeem shares out of the distributable profits or out of the proceeds of a fresh issue of shares made for that purpose. Under certain circumstances private companies may redeem shares out of capital.

  s.687

- Redeemed shares are treated as cancelled on redemption, the amount of the issued share capital being reduced by the nominal value of the shares.

  s.688

Procedure

- The process for the redemption of shares is identical to that for purchase of shares by the company (see page 177).

Filing requirement

- Form SH02 within one month.

More information

Handbook: Chapter 5. Manual: Chapter 8.

Shares – transfer

The transfer of shares in a company is governed by the provisions of the company's articles of association and ss.770 to 782 of the Act.

Companies adopting either of the model articles will not contain any restrictions on the transferability of shares; however, many private companies will adopt pre-emption provisions on the transfer of shares.

Public companies whose shares are publicly traded are not permitted to restrict the transfer of shares, except in a few specified circumstances such as transfers to more than four joint holders, or transfer of shares over which the company has a lien.

Checklist

- Is the transferee a shareholder?
- Is the stock transfer form completed correctly and signed by the transferor?   s.770(1)(a)
- Is the form stamped or certified as exempt?   s.770(1)(b)
- Is the form accompanied by share certificates evidencing title to at least the number of shares being transferred?

Procedure

- The transferor should complete a stock transfer form giving details of the shares to be transferred, their own name and address as transferor and the name and address of the transferee. The form should be signed by the transferor and, where the shares are partly paid, by the transferee.
- Prior to registration by the company it will be necessary for the stock transfer form to be stamped by HM Revenue & Customs (see page 114) unless the transfer is exempt from duty and has been signed and certified on the reverse. Stamp duty is payable by the purchaser of the shares. Duty is due on transfers with a consideration of more than £1,000. The current rate for stamp duty is 0.5 per cent, rounded up to the nearest £5, of the consideration paid or payable (whether or not the consideration is cash).

- The stamped stock transfer form together with the original share certificate should be forwarded to the company or its registrar (as appropriate) for registration.
- Upon receipt of a stock transfer form the company should check that the details of the transferor are correct and that the share certificate is valid. If the original share certificate has been mislaid, it will be necessary for the transferor to complete an indemnity in respect of this lost certificate.
- Many private companies have detailed pre-emption provisions on the transfer of shares, and care must be taken to ensure that these are followed. Alternatively, the pre-emption rights may be waived by the remaining shareholders.
- The transfer of shares requires approval from the board of directors who should also authorise the issue of a share certificate to the transferee and of any balancing certificate to the transferor.
- Details of the transfer must be entered in the register of members.
- Transfers must be processed or rejected within two months of receipt. Where rejected, the reasons for refusal must be provided.   s.771(1)

Filing requirement

- Share transfers are not notified to Companies House; however, details of the transfer must be shown on the company's next annual return.   s.856(3)(b)

More information

📙 Handbook: Chapter 6. 📗 Manual: Chapter 5.

Shares – transmission

Transmission is the process by which title to shares is transferred by operation of law, rather than a sale or transfer by a shareholder. The most common form of transmission of shares is on the death of a shareholder.

Checklist

- Is the transferee a shareholder?
- Is the stock transfer form completed correctly an signed by the executor or personal representative?   s.770(1)(a)
- Is the form stamped or certified as exempt?   s.770(1)(b)
- Is the form accompanied by share certificates evidencing title to at least the number of shares being transferred?

Procedure

- A stock transfer form should be completed giving details of the shares to be transferred, the name and address of the registered holder as transferor, and the name and address of the transferee. The form should be signed by the person lodging the form together with documentary evidence of their authority, such as a grant of probate.
- Prior to registration by the company it will be necessary for the stock transfer form to be stamped by HM Revenue & Customs (see page 114) unless the transfer is exempt from duty and has been signed and certified on the reverse. Most transmissions of shares are not liable to stamp duty and the form should be certified accordingly.
- The (stamped) stock transfer form together with the original share certificate should be forwarded to the company or its registrar (as appropriate) for registration.
- Upon receipt of a stock transfer form the company should check that the details of the transferor are correct and that the share certificate is valid. If the original share certificate has been mislaid, it will be necessary for the transferor to complete an indemnity in respect of this lost certificate.
- Many private companies have detailed pre-emption provisions

on the transfer of shares, and care must be taken to ensure that these are followed. Alternatively, the pre-emption rights may be waived by the remaining shareholders.

■ The transfer of shares requires approval from the board of directors, who should also authorise the issue of a share certificate to the transferee and of any balancing certificate to the transferor.

■ Details of the transfer must be entered in the register of members.

■ Transfers must be processed or rejected within two months of receipt. Where rejected, the reasons for refusal must be provided.   s.771(1)

Filing requirement

■ Share transfers are not notified to Companies House; however, details of the transfer must be shown on the company's next annual return.   s.856(3)(b)

More information

📘 Handbook: Chapters 6 and 8. 📗 Manual: Chapter 5.

Statutory forms and filing periods

Type	Description	CA 2006 Section(s)	Form Code	Filing Period
Dissolution				
	Striking-off application by a company	1003	DS01	
	Withdrawal of striking-off application by a company	1010	DS02	
Adminis-tration Restoration				
	Application for administrative restoration to the Register	1024	RT01	6 years
Change of Constitu-tion				
	Notice of restriction on the company's articles	23	CC01	15 days
	Notice of removal of restriction on the company's articles	23	CC02	15 days
	Statement of compliance where amendment of articles restricted	24	CC03	15 days
	Statement of company's objects	31	CC04	15 days
	Change of constitution by enactment	34	CC05	15 days
	Change of constitution by order of court or other authority	35	CC06	15 days
Re-registration				
	Application by a private company for re-registration as a public company	94 & 765(4)	RR01	15 days
	Application by a public company for re-registration as a private limited company	100	RR02	15 days
	Notice by the company of application to the court for cancellation of resolution for re-registration	99(2)	RR03	Imme-diate notice

Type	Description	CA 2006 Section(s)	Form Code	Filing Period
	Notice by the applicants of application to the court for cancellation of resolution for re-registration	99(1)	RR04	Immediate notice
	Application by a private limited company for re-registration as private unlimited company	103	RR05	15 days
	Application by an unlimited company for re-registration as a private limited company	106	RR06	15 days
	Application by a public company for re-registration as a private unlimited company	110	RR07	15 days
	Application by a public company for re-registration as a private limited company following a court order reducing capital	651	RR08	
	Application by a public company for re-registration as a private company following cancellation of shares	664	RR09	15 days
	Application by a public company for re-registration as a private company following a reduction of capital due to redenomination	766	RR10	15 days
Annual return				
	Annual return	854	AR01	28 days
	Notification of single alternative inspection location (SAIL)	114. 162, 228, 237,	AD02	14 days
	Change of location of company records to the registered office	275, 358, 702, 720, 743, 805,	AD04	14 days
	Change of location of the company records to the SAIL	809, 877& 892	AD03	14 days
Change of name				
	Exemption from requirement as to use of 'limited' or 'cyfyngedig' on change of name	60	NE01	
	Notice of change of name by resolution	78	NM01	15 days
	Notice of change of name by conditional resolution	78	NM02	15 days
	Notice confirming satisfaction of the conditional resolution for change of name	78	NM03	

Type	Description	CA 2006 Section(s)	Form Code	Filing Period
	Notice of change of name by means provided for in the articles	79	NM04	
	Notice of change of name by resolution of directors	64 or 1033	NM05	
	Request to seek comments of government department or other specified body on change of name	56	NM06	
Directors & Secretaries				
	Appointment of director	167	AP01	14 days
	Appointment of corporate director	167	AP02	14 days
	Appointment of secretary	276	AP03	14 days
	Appointment of corporate secretary	276	AP04	14 days
	Termination of appointment of director	167	TM01	14 days
	Termination of appointment of secretary	276	TM02	14 days
	Change of director's details	167	CH01	14 days
	Change of corporate director's details	167	CH02	14 days
	Change of secretary's details	276	CH03	14 days
	Change of corporate secretary's details	276	CH04	14 days
Incorporation				
	Application to register a company	9	IN01	
Registrar's powers				
	Replacement of document not meeting requirements for proper delivery	1076	RP01	
	Application for rectification by the Registrar of Companies	1095	RP02	
	Notice of an objection to a request for the Registrar of Companies to rectify the Register	1095	RP03	
	Certified voluntary translation of an original document that is or has been delivered to the Registrar of Companies	1106	VT01	
	Application by an individual to make an address unavailable for public inspection	1088	SR01	
	Application to make the address unavailable for public inspection for a person who is not currently an officer, but was an officer	1088	SR02	

Type	Description	CA 2006 Section(s)	Form Code	Filing Period
	Application by a company to make an address unavailable for public inspection	1088	SR02	
	Application by a person who registers a charge to make an address unavailable for public inspection	1088	SR03	
Share capital				
	Return of allotment of shares	555	SH01	Within 1 month of allotment
	Notice of consolidation, subdivision, redemption of shares or re-conversion of stock into shares	619, 621 & 689	SH02	within 1 month
	Return of purchase of own shares	707	SH03	28 days
	Notice of sale or transfer of treasury shares for a public limited company (PLC)	728	SH04	28 days
	Notice of cancellation of treasury shares for a public limited company (PLC)	730	SH05	28 days
	Notice of cancellation of shares	708	SH06	28 days
	Notice of cancellation of shares held by or for a public company	663	SH07	1 month
	Notice of name or other designation of class of shares	636	SH08	1 month
	Return of allotment by unlimited company allotting new class of shares	556	SH09	1 month
	Notice of particulars of variation of rights attached to shares	637	SH10	1 month
	Notice of new class of members	638	SH11	1 month
	Notice of particulars of variation of class rights	640	SH12	1 month
	Notice of name or other designation of class of members	639	SH13	1 month
	Notice of redenomination	625	SH14	1 month
	Notice of reduction of capital following redenomination	627	SH15	15 days
	Notice by the applicants of application to court for cancellation of the special resolution approving a redemption or purchase of shares out of capital	722(1)	SH16	Immediate
	Notice by the company of application to court for cancellation of the special resolution approving a redemption or purchase of shares out of capital	722(2)	SH17	Immediate

Type	Description	CA 2006 Section(s)	Form Code	Filing Period
	Statement of directors in respect of the solvency statement made in accordance with s.643	643	SH18	15 days
	Statement of capital	108	SH19	15 days
	Statement of capital	644 & 649	SH19	15 days
	Statement of directors in accordance with reduction of capital following redenomination	627	SH20	15 days
	Application for trading certificate for a public company	761 & 762	SH50	
Liquidation				
	Notice of appointment of an administrative receiver, receiver or manager	871(1)	LQ01	7 days
	Notice of ceasing to act as an administrative receiver, receiver or manager	871(2)	LQ02	
Accounts				
	Change of accounting reference date	392	AA01	Prior to expiry of period for filing accounts
	Dormant company accounts	480	AA02	9 months
	Notice of resolution removing auditors	512	AA03	14 days
	Notice of an application to the court made under s.456(1) and general statement of the matters at issue		AA04	
	Notice of a failed or withdrawn application to the court made under s.456(1)		AA05	
Change of registered office				
	Change of registered office address	87	AD01	Takes effect on delivery
	Notice to change the situation of an England and Wales company or a Welsh company	88	AD05	15 days
Investment companies				
	Notice of intention to carry on business as an investment company	833(1)	IC01	
	Notice that a company no longer wishes to be an investment company	833(4)	IC02	

Type	Description	CA 2006 Section(s)	Form Code	Filing Period
Housing corporation				
	Registration of a company as a social landlord		HC01	
	Removal of a company as social landlord		HC02	
	Notice of appeal against decision to remove a company from the Register of social landlords		HC03	
CICs				
	Notice to the Registrar of Companies by the Regulator of Community Interest Companies of an order appoint a director under s.45(1) of the Companies (Audit, Investigations and Community Enterprise) Act 2004	Section 45(1) of the Companies (Audit, Investigations and Community Enterprise) Act 2004	CI AP01	14 days
	Notice to the Registrar of Companies by the Regulator of Community Interest Companies of an order appoint a corporate director under s.45(1) of the Companies (Audit, Investigations and Community Enterprise) Act 2004	Section 45(1) of the Companies (Audit, Investigations and Community Enterprise) Act 2004	CI AP02	14 days
	Notice to the Registrar of Companies by the Regulator of Community Interest Companies of an order removing a director under s.46(1) of the Companies (Audit, Investigations and Community Enterprise) Act 2004	Section 46(1) of the Companies (Audit, Investigations and Community Enterprise) Act 2004	CI TM01	14 days
	Notice to the Registrar of Companies by the Regulator of Community Interest Companies of an order to suspend a director under s.46(3) of the Companies (Audit, Investigations and Community Enterprise) Act 2004	Section 46(3) of the Companies (Audit, Investigations and Community Enterprise) Act 2004	CI CC01	14 days

Type	Description	CA 2006 Section(s)	Form Code	Filing Period
	Notice to the Registrar of Companies by the Regulator of Community Interest Companies of the termination of appointment of director under s.45(8) of the Companies (Audit, Investigations and Community Enterprise) Act 2004	Section 45(8) of the Companies (Audit, Investigations and Community Enterprise) Act 2004	CI TM02	14 days
EEIGs	EEIG companies			
	Statement of name, official address, members, objects and duration for EEIG whose official address is in the UK		EE FM01	
	Statement of name, establishment address in the UK and members of an EEIG whose official address is outside the UK		EE FM02	
	Appointment of manager of an EEIG where the official address of the EEIG is in the UK		EE AP01	
	Appointment of corporate manager of an EEIG where the official address of the EEIG is in the UK		EE AP02	
	Change of details for a manager of an EEIG where the official address of the EEIG is in the UK		EE CH01	
	Change of details for corporate manager of an EEIG where the official address of the EEIG is in the UK		EE CH02	
	Termination of appointment of manager of an EEIG where the official address is in the UK		EE TM01	
	Statement of name, other than registered name, under which an EEIG, whose official address is outside the UK, proposes to carry on business in the UK		EE NM01	
	Statement of name, other than registered name, under which an EEIG, whose official address is outside the UK, proposes to carry on business in substitution for name previously approved		EE NM02	
	Notice of documents and particulars required to be filed for an EEIG		EE MP01	
	Notice of setting up or closure of an establishment of an EEIG		EE MP02	

Type	Description	CA 2006 Section(s)	Form Code	Filing Period
SEs				
	Appointment of a member of a supervisory organ of a Societas Europaea (SE)		SE AP01	14 days
	Appointment of corporate member of a supervisory organ of Societas Europaea (SE)		SE AP02	14 days
	Terminating appointment of member of a supervisory organ of Societas Europaea (SE)		SE TM01	14 days
	Change of member's details of a supervisory organ of a Societas Europaea (SE)		SE CH01	14 days
	Change of corporate member's details of a supervisory organ of Societas Europaea (SE)		SE CH02	14 days
	Amendment of statutes of Societas Europaea (SE)		SE AS01	14 days
	Conversion of Societas Europaea (SE) to public limited company (PLC)		SE CV01	At least 2 years or 2 sets of accounts
	Draft terms of formation holding Societas Europaea (SE) involving a Great Britain (GB) registered company of SE		SE DT01	
	Draft terms of conversion of public limited company (PLC) to Societas Europaea (SE)		SE DT02	
	Notification of draft terms of conversion of Societas Europaea (SE) to a public limited company (PLC)		SE DT03	
	Formation by merger of Societas Europaea (SE) to be registered in Great Britain (GB)		SE FM01	
	Formation of holding Societas Europaea (SE)		SE FM02	
	Formation of subsidiary Societas Europaea (SE) under Article 2(3) of Council Regulation (EC) No 2157/2001		SE FM03	
	Transformation of a public limited company (PLC) to Societas Europaea (SE)		SE FM04	At least 2 years as subsidiary in another state
	Formation of subsidiary Societas Europaea (SE) under Article 3(2) of Council Regulation (EC) No 2157/2001		SE FM05	

Type	Description	CA 2006 Section(s)	Form Code	Filing Period
	Notice of satisfaction of conditions for the formation of holding Societas Europaea (SE) by a Great Britain (GB) registered company or SE		SE SC01	14 days
	Statement of solvency by members of Societas Europaea (SE) which is proposing to transfer from (Great Britain) GB		SE SS01	
	Proposed transfer from Great Britain (GB) of Societas Europaea (SE) SE68(1) (a)		SE TR01	
	Transfer to Great Britain (GB) of Societas Europaea (SE)		SE TR02	* see below
	Transfer from Great Britain (GB) of Societas Europaea (SE)		SE TR03	* see below
	Notice of initiation or termination of winding up, liquidation, insolvency, cessation of payment procedures and decision to continue operating of Societas Europaea (SE)		SE WU01	
Newspaper forms				
	Return of change in proprietors of a newspaper		NP AP01	
	Initial registration/annual return form for a newspaper		NP AR01	
Non-Companies Act companies				
	Application by a joint stock company for registration as a public company under the Companies Act 2006	1040	NC IN01	
	Application by a joint stock company for registration as a private company under the Companies Act 2006	1040	NC IN02	
	Application by a company (not being a joint stock company) for registration under the Companies Act 2006	1040	NC IN03	
PROOF				
	PROOF: Consent form for paper filing		PR03	

*At least 2 months after a proposal for the transfer has been published.

Type	Description	CA 2006 Section(s)	Form Code	Filing Period
Cross-Border Merger Form				
	Notice of cross-border merger involving a UK-registered company		CB01	2 months before 1st meeting of the members
Opening of Overseas Branch Register				
	Notice of opening of overseas branch register	130	AD06	Within 14 days
	Notice of discontinuance of overseas branch register	135	AD07	Within 14 days
Section 243 Exemption				
	Application under s.243 by an individual	243	SR04	
	Application under s.243 by a company	243	SR05	
	Application under s.243 by a subscriber to a memorandum of association	243	SR06	
	Notice to the Registrar that a decision to refrain from disclosing a director's protected information to credit reference agencies should cease to apply	243	SR07	
Mortgage				
	Particulars of a mortgage or charge	860	MG01	21 days
	Statement of satisfaction in full or in part of mortgage or charge	872(1)(a)	MG02	
	Application for registration of a memorandum of satisfaction that part [or the whole] of the property charged (a) has been released from the charge; (b) no longer forms part of the company's property	872(1)(b)	MG04	
	Particulars of a charge subject to which property has been acquired	862	MG06	21 days
	Particulars for the registration of a charge to secure a series of debentures	863(1)	MG07	21 days
	Particulars of an issue of secured debentures in a series	863(3)	MG08	21 days
	Certificate of registration of a charge comprising property situated in another UK jurisdiction	867(2)	MG09	

Type	Description	CA 2006 Section(s)	Form Code	Filing Period
Scottish mortgage				
	Particulars of a charge created by a company registered in Scotland	878	MG01s	21 days
	Statement of satisfaction in full or in part of a fixed charge for a company registered in Scotland	887(1)(a)	MG02s	
	Statement of satisfaction in full or in part of a floating charge for a company registered in Scotland	887(1)(a) & 887(2)(a) or (b)	MG03s	
	Application for registration of a memorandum of satisfaction that part [or the whole] of the property charged (a) has been released from the fixed charge; (b) no longer forms part of the company's property for a company registered in Scotland.	887(1)(b)	MG04s	
	Application for registration of a memorandum of satisfaction that part [or the whole] of the property charged (a) has been released from the floating charge; (b) no longer forms part of the company's property for a company registered in Scotland.	887(1)(b) & 887(2)(a) or (b)	MG05s	
	Particulars of a charge subject to which property has been acquired by a company registered in Scotland	880	MG06s	21 days
	Particulars for the registration of a charge to secure a series of debentures by a company registered in Scotland	882(1)	MG07s	21 days
	Particulars of an issue of secured debentures in a series by a company registered in Scotland	882(3)	MG08s	21 days
LLPs				
	Application for the incorporation of a limited liability partnership (LLP)		LL IN01	
	Appointment of member of a limited liability partnership (LLP)		LL AP01	14 days
	Appointment of corporate member of a limited liability partnership (LLP)		LL AP02	14 days
	Change of member's details of a limited liability partnership (LLP)		LL CH01	28 days
	Change of corporate member's details of a limited liability partnership (LLP)		LL CH02	28 days

Type	Description	CA 2006 Section(s)	Form Code	Filing Period
	Termination of appointment of member of a limited liability partnership (LLP)		LL TM01	14 days
	Change of accounting reference date of a limited liability partnership (LLP)		LL AA01	Before deadline for filing accounts has expired
	Notice of removal of auditors from a limited liability partnership (LLP)		LL AA02	
	Change of registered office address of a limited liability partnership (LLP)		LL AD01	
	Notification of the single alternative inspection location (SAIL) of a limited liability partnership (LLP)		LL AD02	
	Change of location of records to the single alternative inspection location (SAIL) of a limited liability partnership (LLP)		LL AD03	
	Change of location of records to the registered office of a limited liability partnership (LLP)		LL AD04	
	Notice to change the situation of an England and Wales limited liability partnership or a Welsh limited liability partnership (LLP)		LL AD05	
	Annual return of a limited liability partnership (LLP)		LL AR01	28 days
	Notice of change of status of a limited liability partnership (LLP)		LL DE01	
	Notice of change of name of a limited liability partnership (LLP)		LL NM01	
	Striking off of a limited liability partnership (LLP)		LL DS01	
	Withdrawal of striking off application by a limited liability partnership (LLP)		LL DS02	
	Notice of appointment of an administrative receiver, receiver or manager by a limited liability partnership (LLP)		LL LQ01	7 days
	Notice of ceasing to act as an administrative receiver, receiver or manager by a limited liability partnership (LLP)		LL LQ02	

Type	Description	CA 2006 Section(s)	Form Code	Filing Period
	Replacement of document not meeting requirements for proper delivery for a limited liability partnership (LLP)		LL RP01	
	Application for rectification by the Registrar of Companies for a limited liability partnership (LLP)		LL RP02	
	Notice of an objection to a request for the Registrar of Companies to rectify the Register for a limited liability partnership (LLP)		LL RP03	
	Certified voluntary translation of an original document that is or has been delivered to the Registrar of Companies for a limited liability partnership (LLP)		LL VT01	
	Application for administrative restoration of a limited liability partnership (LLP) to the Register		LL RT01	
LLP mortgage				
	Particulars of a mortgage or charge in respect of a limited liability partnership (LLP)		LL MG01	21 days
	Statement of satisfaction by a limited liability partnership (LLP) in full or part of mortgage or charge		LL MG02	
	Application for registration of a memorandum of satisfaction that part. [or the whole] of the property charged (a) has been released from the charge, (b) no longer forms part of the limited liability partnership's (LLP) property		LL MG04	
	Particulars of charge subject to which property has been acquired by a limited liability partnership (LLP)		LL MG06	21 days
	Particulars for the registration of a charge to secure a series of debentures by a limited liability partnership (LLP)		LL MG07	21 days
	Particulars of an issue of secured debentures in a series by a limited liability partnership (LLP)		LL MG08	21 days
	Certificate of registration by a limited liability partnership (LLP) of a charge comprising property situated in another UK jurisdiction		LL MG09	21 days

Type	Description	CA 2006 Section(s)	Form Code	Filing Period
* LLP Scottish mortgage				
	Particulars of a charge created by a limited liability partnership (LLP) registered in Scotland		LL MG01s	21 days
	Statement of satisfaction in full or part of a fixed charge by a limited liability partnership (LLP) registered in Scotland		LL MG02s	
	Statement of satisfaction in full or part of a floating charge by a limited liability partnership (LLP) registered in Scotland		LL MG03s	
	Application for registration of a memorandum of satisfaction that part [or the whole] of the property charged (a) has been released from the fixed charge, (b) no longer forms part of the limited liability partnership's (LLP) property by an LLP registered in Scotland		LL MG04s	
	Application for registration of a memorandum of satisfaction that part [or the whole] of the property charged (a) has been released from the floating charge; (b) no longer forms part of the limited liability partnership's (LLP) property for an LLP registered in Scotland		LL MG05s	
	Particulars of a charge subject to which property has been acquired by a limited liability partnership (LLP) registered in Scotland		LL MG06s	21 days
	Particulars for the registration of a charge to secure a series of debentures by a limited liability partnership (LLP) registered in Scotland		LL MG07s	21 days
	Particulars of an issue of secured debentures in a series in respect by a limited liability partnership (LLP) registered in Scotland		LL MG08s	21 days

* Information taken from the LLP Act 2000 and CA 2006 where applicable.

Type	Description	CA 2006 Section(s)	Form Code	Filing Period
Other appoint-ments				
	Appointment of a manager under s.47 of the Companies (Audit, Investigations and Community Enterprise) Act 2004 or receiver and manager under s.18 of the Charities Act 1993 or judicial factor (Scotland)	1154	AP05	14 days
	Termination of appointment of manager under s.47 of the Companies (Audit, Investigations and Community Enterprise) Act 2004 or receiver and manager under s.18 of the Charities Act 1993 or Judicial Factor (Scotland)	1154	TM03	14 days
	Change of service address for manager appointed under s.47 of the Companies (Audit, Investigations and Community Enterprise) Act 2004 or receiver and manager under s.18 of the Charities Act 1993 or judicial factor (Scotland)	1154	CH05	14 days
* Overseas				
	Registration of an overseas company opening a UK establishment		OS IN01	1 month
	Registration of change of name of overseas company as registered in the UK		OS NM01	21 days
	Notice by an overseas company of change of corporate name in country of incorporation that is registered with an alternative name in the UK		OS NM02	21 days
	Return by an overseas company of an alteration to constitutional documents		OS CC01	21 days
	Return by an overseas company of change of UK establishment at which the constitutional documents are kept		OS AD01	21 days
	Notice of location or change in location of instruments creating charges and register of charges for an overseas company		OS AD02	
	Appointment of director of an overseas company		OS AP01	21 days
	Appointment of secretary of an overseas company		OS AP03	21 days

* Information taken from the Draft Overseas Companies Regulations 2009.

Type	Description	CA 2006 Section(s)	Form Code	Filing Period
	Appointment of corporate director of an overseas company		OS AP02	21 days
	Appointment of corporate secretary of an overseas company		OS AP04	21 days
	Appointment by an overseas company of a person authorised to represent the company as a permanent representative in respect of a UK establishment		OS AP05	21 days
	Appointment of a Judicial factor (Scotland) for an overseas company		OS AP06	14 days
	Appointment by an overseas company of a person authorised to accept service of documents on behalf of the company in respect of a UK establishment		OS AP07	21 days
	Termination of appointment of director of an overseas company		OS TM01	21 days
	Termination of appointment of secretary of an overseas company		OS TM02	21 days
	Termination of appointment by an overseas company of a person authorised to accept services or person authorised to represent the company in respect of a UK establishment		OS TM03	21 days
	Termination of appointment of Judicial Factor (Scotland) of an overseas company		OS TM04	
	Return by a UK establishment of an overseas company for change of details		OS CH01	21 days
	Return by an overseas company for change of company details		OS CH02	21 days
	Change of director's details of an overseas company		OS CH03	21 days
	Change of corporate director's details of an overseas company		OS CH04	21 days
	Change of secretary's details of an overseas company		OS CH05	21 days
	Change of corporate secretary's details of an overseas company		OS CH06	21 days
	Change of details by an overseas company for a person authorised to represent the company in respect of a UK establishment		OS CH07	21 days

Type	Description	CA 2006 Section(s)	Form Code	Filing Period
	Change of service address for a Judicial factor (Scotland) of an overseas company		OS CH08	
	Change of details by an overseas company for a person authorised to accept service of documents on behalf of the company in respect of a UK establishment		OS CH09	21 days
	Notice of closure of a UK establishment of an overseas company		OS DS01	Forth-with
	Notice of termination of winding up of an overseas company		OS DS02	14 days
	Notice of appointment of a liquidator of an overseas company		OS LQ01	1 month/ 14 days
	Notice by an overseas company which becomes subject to proceedings relating to insolvency		OS LQ02	1 month/ 14 days
	Notice of winding-up of an overseas company		OS LQ03	1 month/ 14 days
	Notice by an overseas company on cessation of proceedings relating to insolvency		OS LQ04	14 days from date cease to be subject to proceed-ings
	Particulars of a mortgage or charge of an overseas company		OS MG01	21 days
Disqualified directors forms				
	Disqualification order against an individual		DQ 01	
	Disqualification undertakings given by an individual		DQ 02	
	Grant of leave in relation to a disqualification order or disqualification undertaking		DQ 03	
	Variation or cessation of a disqualification order or disqualification undertaking		DQ 04	
	Disqualification order against a corporate body or firm		DQ 05	
	Disqualification undertaking given by a corporate body or firm		DQ 06	

Type	Description	CA 2006 Section(s)	Form Code	Filing Period
Disqualified directors forms Northern Ireland				
	Disqualification order against an individual in Northern Ireland		DQ 01n	
	Disqualification undertakings given by an individual in Northern Ireland		DQ 02n	
	Grant of leave in relation to a disqualification order or disqualification undertaking in Northern Ireland		DQ 03n	
	Variation or cessation of a disqualification order or disqualification undertaking in Northern Ireland		DQ 04n	
	Disqualification order against a corporate body or firm in Northern Ireland		DQ 05n	
	Disqualification undertaking given by a corporate body or firm in Northern Ireland		DQ 06n	
Bilingual forms				
	Appointment of director	167	AP01c	14 days
	Appointment of corporate director	167	AP02c	14 days
	Appointment of secretary	276	AP03c	14 days
	Appointment of corporate secretary	276	AP04c	14 days
	Change of director's details	167	CH01c	14 days
	Change of corporate director's details	167	CH02c	14 days
	Change of secretary's details	276	CH03c	14 days
	Change of corporate secretary's details	276	CH04c	14 days
	Termination of appointment of director	167	TM01c	14 days
	Termination of appointment of secretary	276	TM02c	14 days
	Change of accounting reference date		AA01c	Prior to expiry of period for filing accounts
	Dormant company accounts on or after 6/4/08		AA02c	9 months
	Annual returns		AR01c	28 days
	Return of allotment of shares		SH01c	1 month

Type	Description	CA 2006 Section(s)	Form Code	Filing Period
	Application for registration of a company		IN01c	On application
	Exemption from requirement as to the use of 'limited' or 'cyfyngedig' on change of name		NE01c	
	Notice of change of name by resolution		NM01c	15 days
	Change of registered office address		AD01c	Takes effect on delivery
	Notice to change the situation of a Welsh/England and Wales company		AD05c	15 days
	Striking off application by a company (and continuation page)		DS01c	
	Withdrawal of striking off application by a company		DS02c	
	Change of accounting reference date of a LLP		LL AA01c	Prior to expiry of period for filing accounts
	Change of registered office of a LLP		LL AD01c	
	Notice to change the situation of a Welsh/England and Wales LLP		LL AD05c	
	Appointment of member		LL AP01c	14 days
	Appointment of corporate member		LLAP02c	14 days
	Change of member's details		LL CH01c	28 days
	Change of corporate member's details		LL CH02c	28 days
	Termination of appointment of a member		LL TM01c	14 days
	Annual return (and continuation pages)		LL AR01c	28 days
	Notice of designated member(s) of an LLP		LL DE01c	14 days
	Application for incorporation of an LLP		LL IN01c	
	Notice of change of name of an LLP		LL NM01c	
	Striking-off of an LLP (and continuation page)		LL DS01c	
	Withdrawal of striking off of an LLP		LL DS02c	

Statutory registers and records

The Companies Act requires the following registers to be kept by all companies:

- Register of members.   s.113
- Register of charges.   s.876 or s.891
- Minute books of the proceedings of meetings of the shareholders   ss.355, 248 and its directors and of any sub-committees of the directors.
- Accounting records.   s.386
- Register of directors.   s.162
- Register of directors' usual residential addresses   s.165
- Copies of directors' service contracts or memorandum of terms   s.228
- Copies of any indemnity provisions for directors   s.237
- Register of secretaries   s.275
- If the company is a public company, register of interests in   s.808 voting shares.
- Copies of contracts for market and off market purchases of own   s.702 shares
- Directors' and auditors' statements in relation to purchase of   s.720 shares by a private company out of capital
- Reports into investigation of ownership of shares   s.805
- Although not required by the Act, if the company maintains a   s.743 register of debenture holders, there are requirements laid down by the Act governing its maintenance and inspection.

Checklist

- The following rules apply to all the company's statutory registers and records.
- These must all be kept at the registered office or at an alternative   s.1186 place of inspection details of which must be notified to Companies House on form AD02.

Filing requirement

- Forms AD02, AD03 or AD04.

More information

Handbook: Chapter 12.   Manual: Chapter 9.

Treasury shares

s.724

Companies whose shares are listed or admitted to AIM or an equivalent regulated market in the EEA may acquire their own shares and hold these in treasury. Unlike the existing provisions relating to purchase of own shares (see page 177), shares purchased under the treasury shares provisions are not cancelled on purchase but may be retained, or sold.

Checklist

- Are the shares qualifying shares? s.724(2)
- Does the company have sufficient distributable profit? s.724(1)(b)
- Does the company have sufficient cash resources?
- Check that the articles permit the purchase of its own shares by the company.

Procedure

- The general procedure for the purchase by a company of its own shares is set out on pages 177–179.
- Once the company has purchased the shares to be held in treasury, a return on form SH03 must be submitted to the Registrar, stating the number of shares and the class of shares, together with the nominal value of the shares and the date on which they were re-purchased. The purchase of shares to be held in treasury by a company is subject to stamp duty, the duty being payable where the aggregate consideration exceeds £1,000 and not the nominal value, at the rate of 0.5 per cent (rounded up to the nearest £5). s.707
- If the shares are subsequently cancelled, sold or transferred, form SH04 or SH05 must be filed. ss.727, 728, 729

Filing requirement

- Copy of ordinary resolution.
- Form SH03.
- Form SH04, SH05 within 28 days of cancellation, sale or transfer.

Notes

- If a company holding shares in treasury ceases to qualify to hold   s.727
treasury shares, any shares held in treasury are cancelled.
- Shares held in treasury may be sold for cash, transferred to
satisfy claims under employee share schemes, or be cancelled.
- Shares held in treasury have no voting or dividend rights but   s.726
may take up rights in respect of bonus issues and may be
redeemed if the shares are redeemable.
- A maximum of 10 per cent of the issued shares of any class may   s.725(2), (3)
be held in treasury at any time.

More information

Handbook: Chapter 6. Manual: Chapters 5 and 7.

Useful websites

Government sites

BIS (Department for Business Innovation & Skills)	www.berr.gov.uk
Charity Commission	www.charity-commission.gov.uk
Companies House	www.companies-house.gov.uk
Customs & Excise	www.hmce.gov.uk
HM Land Registry	www.landreg.gov.uk
HM Revenue & Customs	www.hmrc.gov.uk
Office of Fair Trading	www.oft.gov.uk
Patent/Trademark Office	www.patent.gov.uk
Public Service Information	www.direct.gov.uk
Stationery Office	www.opsi.gov.uk

Professional bodies

Association of Chartered Certified Accountants	www.acca.org.uk
Chamber of Commerce	www.chambersonline.co.uk
Chartered Institute of Building	www.ciob.org.uk
Chartered Institute of Management Accountants	www.cimaglobal.com
Chartered Institute of Marketing	www.cim.co.uk
Confederation of British Industry	www.cbi.org.uk
Institute of Chartered Accountants in England and Wales	www.icaew.co.uk
Institute of Chartered Accountants in Ireland	www.icai.ie
Institute of Chartered Accountants in Scotland	www.icas.org.uk
Institute of Chartered Secretaries and Administrators	www.icsa.org.uk
Institute of Directors	www.iod.co.uk
The Law Society	www.lawsociety.org.uk
The Law Society of Scotland	www.lawscot.org.uk
Trade Union Congress	www.tuc.org.uk

Other

European Business Registry	www.ebr.org
European Patent Office	www.european-patent-office.org
Nominet UK	www.nominet.net

Waiver of dividend

Occasionally, particularly with private family-owned companies, shareholders will elect to waive entitlement to receive dividends in respect of one or more financial years. This is commonly used where shares are held by a nominee to satisfy a minimum number of shareholder requirements in the articles and thus the nominee will elect not to receive dividends.

Checklist

- Waiver must pre-date date of declaration of dividend.

Procedure

- The shareholder will complete a formal letter of waiver under seal or witnessed and will lodge this with the company.
- Often waivers will be restricted to any dividends paid in respect of stated period rather than undated as the waiver is irrevocable.

Filing requirement

- None.

More information

Handbook: Chapter 7. Manual: Chapter 7.